W9-AMA-619

naked reading

Uncovering What Tweens Need to Become Lifelong Readers

WEB... DISCARDED
P.O. ... 69
MARSHFIELD, MO 65706
WCL

TERI S. LESESNE

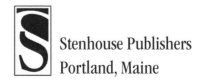

Stenhouse Publishers
Portland, Maine

Stenhouse Publishers
www.stenhouse.com

Copyright © 2006 by Teri Lesesne

All rights reserved. No part of this publication may be reproduced or transmitted in any form or by any means, electronic or mechanical, including photocopy, or any information storage and retrieval system, without permission from the publisher.

Every effort has been made to contact copyright holders and students for permission to reproduce borrowed material. We regret any oversights that may have occurred and will be pleased to rectify them in subsequent reprints of the work.

Library of Congress Cataloging-in-Publication Data
Naked reading : uncovering what tweens need to become lifelong readers / Teri Lesesne.
    p. cm.
    ISBN 1-57110-416-X
    1. Preteens--Books and reading--United States. 2. School children--Books and reading--United States. 3. Middle school students--Books and reading--United States. 4. Reading promotion--United States. 5. Children's literature--Bibliography. 6. Young adult literature--Bibliography.

Z1037.A1L48 2006
328.5'5--dc22   2005057509

Cover, interior design and typeset by studio 7 design
Cover image from Veer/Lene Bladbjerg

Manufactured in the United States of America on acid-free paper
11 10 09 08 07   9 8 7 6 5 4 3

To Dad from "The Doc"

WEBSTER COUNTY LIBRARY
P.O. BOX 89
MARSHFIELD, MO 65706

contents

acknowledgments

My mother and stepfather lived just long enough to see the publication of my first book. Larry, my "Poppa," attended my first-ever book signing at a local Barnes & Noble. Mother could not be there because, as we discovered that day, her cancer had returned. But she dutifully sent Larry to the store with a long list of all the relatives and friends who needed me to autograph a copy of my book. She still might hold the record for number of books sold to one person. I am eternally grateful that she had her own copy and that it showed signs that she had read beyond the opening pages.

It was only after my mother's death that I began to think more deeply about the roots of my own literacy. If I were a student in today's classrooms, I would be given the label "at-risk." I grew up in a single-parent household, one barely above the poverty level at times. While there was little money for extras, my mother knew the importance of books and reading. I suspect that is the reason my sisters and I share a book bond. We give books as presents, have worked in bookstores, are avid readers, and donate books to libraries and shelters once we are done with them.

The one memory of my childhood that stands out time after time is taking the streetcar every two weeks on a Saturday morning to the Carnegie Library in downtown Pittsburgh. We lived on the other side of town, so this was a long trip by my childhood standards. Once I arrived in those hallowed halls of the Carnegie Library, I was permitted to check out a grand total of five books, most of which I had read by the time we got back home. I read and reread these books until the next visit to the library. I remember when I graduated from the children's room and was allowed access to the grown-up books, too. If I close my eyes, I can still see the entrance to this magnificent library with its burnished wood walls and towering dinosaur skeletons. Imagine my chagrin when I discovered that not all libraries have dinosaurs to greet you. One thing they did have in common, though, was wonderful librarians and tons of books that lured me back again and again.

What my mother did was help a new reader find tons of material to entertain and enlighten her. She could not buy me all the books I wanted (but I recall a magical Christmas when I received the complete set of the Nancy Drew *and* the Cherry Ames series books), but she made sure there was plenty to read at home beyond the Dick and Jane basals and her *True Confessions* magazines (which I routinely read on the sly, if truth be told). She helped make me into the reader I am today. In turn, I provide my three grandchildren with books, visits to the library, and trips to my office to search for more books. As I open the boxes of books sent to me by publishers, I make stacks for each child. Natalie, the youngest, squealed with delight this week when I brought home a newly issued paperback trilogy. She read Book One the first night.

Parents can do a lot to assist children in becoming lifetime readers. Sadly, parents who did not have role models might not be able to model for their own children. So it falls to us as educators to provide the models students need. The fact that you have purchased this book proves that you have more than a passing interest in creating lifetime readers in your classroom. I suspect that, like me, someone brought the wonderful world of reading into your life. It might have been a parent or a teacher. It may have happened when you were a small child or perhaps you came to a love of books and reading later in life. Someone gave you the right book at the right time and here you are today attempting to make that match for your students. I hope this book helps you in your endeavors.

No writing is ever done alone; no work emerges from within without a lot of encouragement and assistance. I owe an incredible debt to the many people who helped me in the writing of this book. First, huge thanks go to my family. My mother and stepfather were incredibly supportive of my attempts at writing early on. Mother was one of my best proofreaders, finding errors (alas) in already published articles. My beloved stepfather, Larry, was a constant force of security and stability in my life. I miss them both and wish they were here to read this book, too. My sisters, Jo Ann, Ruth, and Mary Pat, not only encouraged me, but actively spread the word about my book and functioned as a surrogate sales force. As always, I relied on stories and anecdotes from my own grandchildren. Thanks to Cali, Corrie, and Natalie for being so willing to let their Nana tell the world about their exploits with books and reading. My husband wrangled the kids from swim team to band practice to school to who knows where so that I could stay home and do some writing. He would relate stories of the kids that he thought had a place in the book. Thanks, Henry, for helping me spread my wings and fly away from time to time. But, also, thanks for keeping me grounded when I needed to attend to the more important matters of home and heart.

To my extended family at Sam Houston State University's Department of Library Science, I also owe thanks. They championed my first book, proudly displayed copies to all visitors, and even made it one of the textbooks required for some courses. Thanks to Mary Berry, Mary Ann Bell, Rosemary Chance, Frank Hoffmann, Sara Catherine Howard, Robin Krig, Holly Weimar, Joanna Fountain, and Cindy Traylor. And, to my students Cindy, Amy, Esmeralda, Kem, and others: thanks for sharing your students' thoughts with me to help me better understand tweens. How nice it is to have a job where I actually look forward to coming to the office and spending time with colleagues who exhibit a communal sense of purpose and a shared sense of humor.

To my family at Stenhouse, thanks will never suffice. Once again my editor, Bill Varner, managed to convince me I had more to say and then gave me free reign to find my voice. Bill knows how to get more out of me than even I think I have inside. Whenever he would send me comments about the book, I knew it would be something to consider and mull and work over until it found its way into the pages of this book. Stenhouse feels like family because all the folks there support and encourage their authors. Thanks to the people who take the orders, the staff that keeps track of my schedule and makes sure books are there where I am, and all who work hard to provide the best teaching tools available. Thanks to Janet Allen once again for making the match between me and this incredible publishing family.

I need to say thanks to the tremendous research conducted by Karen Gibson and Vickey Giles, former doctoral students at the University of Houston. Their studies into what motivates students were an incredible source of information for me. Dr. Gibson's and Dr. Giles' work is essential for anyone working with kids and reading. Lois Buckman helped in compiling the missing information for the bibliography found in Appendix A. It's good when your best pal is a librarian, too. I appreciate her assistance, especially her willingness to spend time sitting in front of the computer searching for what I needed.

Special thanks to the professional families that have made me a part of their organizations. The National Council of Teachers of English (NCTE), especially the middle-level section, provided some of the information about what tweens want and need for Chapter 2. The Assembly on Literature for Adolescents of NCTE (ALAN), Special Interest Group Network on Adolescent Literature (SIGNAL), and Young Adult Library Services Association (YALSA) and its leaders provide annual workshops and conferences, which present opportunities to meet and know the foremost figures in the field of young adult (YA) literature. They have welcomed me as part of their professional families and helped me hone my thinking about the issues this book tackles.

Finally, my own teachers deserve more than simple acknowledgment; they deserve credit for helping me even reach the point where I believed I could write. Special thanks to Dr. Richard F. Abrahamson, University of Houston, whose mentoring and friendship have shaped my career as a teacher. Dick's wisdom and encouragement means more to me than I can say. I still want to be like him when I finally grow up! To Sr. Melanie DiPietro, English teacher extraordinaire, thanks for teaching that sophomore student how to construct elegant sentences all those years ago. I hope I am fulfilling the promise you saw in me then. Jo Ellen Cullison was my supervising teacher back in my undergraduate days. She remains a champion of my writing and my work. Thanks, Jo Ellen! And because I learn from all those whose work I read and admire, thanks to Janet Allen, Kylene Beers, C. J. Bott, Bob Probst, and Linda Rief. Kylene deserves some singling out since she was always open to listening to me as I bounced ideas off her incredible brain. Some of the ideas in Chapter 5 are adaptations of her strategies for struggling readers. Thanks for the huge assistance there, Kylene. One more nod out to Pam Muñoz Ryan, whose seemingly innocent remark about the title of this book and what she took for its meaning helped me shape the journey for us all. Thanks, Pam!

introduction

We call it naked reading in our house. Let me explain. At age eight or so, my youngest granddaughter, Natalie, picked up on my habit of reading in the bathroom. When you live in a busy house—four women, one guy, and two bathrooms, time spent in that particular room is priceless. For years, I have been a bathroom reader. It is a perfect place for my own personal DEAR (Drop Everything and Read) program. My bathroom is quiet, air-conditioned, and most important, has a lock on the door. And so, for ten to fifteen minutes each morning I would steal away for some quiet reading time. Natalie noticed that I kept books in the bathroom and asked if she could do the same. I was happy to accommodate this request. It just meant adding a magazine rack where she could stow her bathroom book when it was not in her hands. Natalie's routine now when she is called to come and take her bath for the evening is to have her own personal DEAR time (generally fifteen to twenty minutes) before one of us gently reminds her to get into the shower. For the longest time, my husband and I were puzzled about why it took Nat so long to dry off, climb into her pj's, and rejoin the rest of the family. Then one night her sister accidentally let slip the secret: naked reading. Natalie would dive into the walk-in closet in her room, sit down on her little stepstool, and continue to read. When we asked Natalie about this less-than-conventional style of reading, she promptly and earnestly informed us that she had read somewhere that allowing one's body to dry naturally was better for the skin. So, naked reading was born. It took me by surprise at first, but as I considered Natalie and her deep love of books and reading, it made perfect sense.

She was simply finding the time to read without interruption. If only *my* closet were large enough for naked reading.

I had a title for this book early on in the process. It was a great title with a wonderful story behind it. I also knew what the central questions at the heart of the book would be: Why does someone like Natalie love reading so much that she can forget she is naked for thirty to sixty minutes each night? What led her to this total immersion in reading? How could her story help teachers who would love to have kids like Natalie in class? Natalie's naked reading meant more, then. It meant stripping away all the inaccessible language and talking about reading in simple terms in an attempt not only to make reading accessible to reluctant tweens, but to demystify the classroom practices and strategies that can assist teachers in creating their own naked readers. It is important to talk about how to create readers who read outside of school and class requirements; in other words, lifetime readers.

I came to write this book because I know from school visits and from the reports of my own kids that Natalie is a bit of an aberration: at thirteen, she still loves to read. When I began my career as a middle school teacher, most of my students were still avid readers in seventh and eighth grade. Now, teachers of third, fourth, and fifth graders are reporting a startling lack of interest in reading. Recent statistics bear this observation out. The National Assessment for Educational Progress (NAEP) statistics for the years spanning 1979–2001 demonstrate that the percentage of students who report reading for pleasure outside school steadily declined over the 20-plus year span. Kids are opting out of reading earlier and earlier. Oh, they are still what Jim Trelease labels "school-time" readers. They read the assigned texts. But outside the school setting very few find time for pleasure reading. How sad to think that we are losing a generation of readers. How sad—not just because I am a lover of books and want everyone to share my passion, but because lifetime readers, those who read not because they are forced to but because they still want to, are also lifetime learners. If we lose a generation of readers, we also lose a generation of learners. Since today's intermediate and middle school kids are tomorrow's legislators, tomorrow's workforce, and tomorrow's parents, their lack of interest in books and reading and learning will affect subsequent generations. It is enough to make you, like me, determined to reignite a passion for reading.

Why, you might ask, a separate book just for tweens and reading? The answer is that this particular age group is a tough one to tackle in terms of books and reading. They are somewhere between little kids and teens, hence the term *tween*. They will reject books for younger readers such as picture books, and yet many are not quite developmentally ready for the intense experience of reading a YA novel designed for more mature readers. So part of the problem with tweens and reading is locating appropriate material that is interesting to them. In the first couple of chapters, then, we take a look at where these tweens are in terms of their intellectual, emotional, moral, and social development. After that bit of background, we delve into the books themselves. What is out there for this group? What can we offer tweens who are good readers? Struggling readers? Unmotivated readers? Finally, we take a look at how to follow up that reading with some ideas of strategies and activities to connect tweens to their books and reading.

Before we enter into the world of the tween, it is important to examine the definition of reading that I bring to the discussion. Others would frame the discussion of reading in terms of individual skills and strategies. I am not talking about the mechanics of reading: sounding out words, decoding, basic comprehension, and the like. I am talking about reading from an interactive model, reading as a process that requires the reader to be engaged with the text—to transact with the words on the page, in the words of Louise Rosenblatt (1996).

When we uncover a rare item at an antique store, it frequently requires that we strip away years of paint and finish that have marred the natural beauty of the original surface. The same is true for reading. Over the years, we add coat after coat of material that dulls the natural beauty of the act. So, I would like to begin our exploration of naked reading by stripping away some layers of myths that underscore the basic themes of this book.

Exploding Some Myths About Reading

Myth 1: Kids must read only "good" books and not be allowed to wallow in popular fiction. WRONG! We all have an appetite for some food that is not good for us. We all share some guilty pleasure when it comes to reading and books, some book that is not *literary.* We must extend the same courtesy to our students. See the discussion of subliterature in Chapter 2. There is another myth that generally follows from this one: It is not quantity but quality that matters in reading. WRONG! How much we read does matter. Take these statistics from NAEP, the National Assessment of Educational Progress:

Achievement Percentile	Amount of Outside Reading in Minutes/Day	Word Gain/Yr
90th %ile	40+ min/day	2.3 million
50th %ile	<13 min/day	600,000
10th %ile	<2 min/day	51,000

Myth 2: Readers are easy to spot; they always have their noses in books. WRONG! Readers go dormant from time to time. Weeks pass without my picking up a book due to my schedule or my level of fatigue. Kids are no different. And not all readers select books to read, either. They may prefer magazines, comics, or even e-books. Sometimes it is tough to spot the readers. Occasionally, someone who presents as a nonreader is actually a reader between books.

Myth 3: Readability (reading level, lexiles, etc.) is a good way to match books to kids. WRONG! Many of the adult bestsellers I have enjoyed recently are well below my reading level. *Life of Pi* hovers around the fifth-grade level, by the way. *Lemony Snicket* has a higher readability. Scientific formulas applied to the artistic process just do not yield consistent results. If we limit kids to zones of reading or certain levels of books, we might just miss the chance to make the match.

Myth 4: Canned reading programs can create readers. WRONG, so wrong! There is nothing you can buy that will create a reader except the right book for that child. Canned reading programs are management tools at best. They do little or nothing to motivate readers or to create an extrinsic value for reading in kids.

Myth 5: Once kids are independent readers, reading aloud and shared and paired reading should become activities and strategies of the past. WRONG again! See the research conducted by Giles (2005) and Gibson (2004) for a nice counter to this myth.

Myth 6: Kids can automatically distinguish between good and bad literature. WRONG in so many ways. Oh, were this true for adults as well! We would not be plagued with "celebrity" books by Madonna, Katie Couric, Maria Shriver, Dom Deluise, Michael Bolton, Jerry Seinfeld, and others. I prefer to use such books to teach kids and adults how to tell the good from the bad.

Myth 7: Reading is a science that can be broken down into component parts easily for quick consumption. Hello . . . WRONG-O! If reading were a simple act with simple component parts, all of us would learn to read in the same way at the same time with the same level of skill. Hence, any legislation that begins with the phrase, "All children will," is considered suspect. If teachers wrote the opening phrase it would read more along the lines of, "Some children might."

Myth 8: Reading is the same no matter what we are reading or why. So WRONG it is almost laughable. Content-area reading requires specialized content skills. Reading a poem demands a different set of skills from reading directions on programming your cell phone. See Janet Allen's *Tools for Teaching Content Literacy* (2004) and Kylene Beers' *When Kids Can't Read: What Teachers Can Do* (2003) for ideas in content-area strategies.

Myth 9: Having grade-level lists is a good idea. Where do I begin with the WRONGness here? There is no such creature as a fourth-grade book. There are books that might appeal to some fourth graders, but might be just as likely to appeal to some third or even sixth graders. As a middle school teacher I recall near-open warfare when we dared introduce kids in eighth grade to Shakespeare. High school teachers quickly informed us that Shakespeare belonged to them. "Bah, humbug!" as Dickens might retort.

Myth 10: One size fits all, and the corollary: one book is good for all kids. Yes, this, too, is WRONG. The phenomenon of Harry Potter might lead some of us to conclude that there can be one book that will appeal equally to all kids. However, there are some aesthetes, though few, who do not care for Rowling's magical tales. Ditto folks who never watch reality shows. Tastes differ, and we need to offer a variety of reading fare for all tastes. Books need to be sweet, frothy desserts as well as hearty, meaty main courses. My hope is that this book, with the extensive list in the appendix, offers a wide range of choice delectables to sate all reading palates.

chapter 1

Naked Reading:
The Bare Essentials

Quick Takes: Brad and Andrew, age ten

Brad is a gifted reader. He has already left behind the short chapter books that are still popular with many of his classmates, favoring instead the complex fantasies of Brian Jacques' Redwall books. Brad reads at every available moment though his life is fairly full of other activities: soccer, piano lessons, and play dates among them. He often will stay up late at night reading, even after repeated requests to turn out the lights. If he has a spare moment, there will be a book in his hand. He reads while he absently munches his cereal in the morning, takes a book along on the bus ride to school, and has been known to carry a book to church on Sunday—in his words, "just in case" (of course, he is astonished when his parents ask him to leave the book behind in the car). Brad is one of those wonderful kids each and every one of us love to find: he is already a lifetime reader. The challenge with Brad is not motivating him to read. The challenge is to find new books for him as he devours book after book. In some ways, this challenge is just as daunting. Brad is ten, and the books he reads still need to be appropriate for someone of his developmental level. While Brad's vocabulary far outstrips those of other ten-year-olds and he can access more difficult text, he still is not ready for books that explore topics and subjects and issues beyond his moral, emotional, and social development. Brad's teachers and his librarian are kept busy trying to keep him supplied with enough books.

Compare Brad with Andrew, age ten, who tells me, "I do not like to read because I cannot read very good. I guess I am a picky reader because I like some things like biographies of Jerry Rice. I like to finish books but not start them. I also like mysteries and books with facts about animals and sports." Andrew is a reluctant reader. When he finds books about subjects he likes, he tends to pick them up and read them, though he remarks that he likes to finish books but not start them. He even notes that he tries to read twenty pages a day when the book is long but he is interested in it. Andrew has learned how to cope with his reluctance to read by setting reading goals, by selecting books of interest, and by understanding his own tastes and preferences in reading. Andrew has, of course, been helped in his struggles by some outstanding teachers and librarians, who have taken the time to discover his interests and preferences in life and who try to relate those to the books recommended for reading. Andrew and Brad are the same age and gender yet there exists between them a huge chasm in terms of books and reading. This is just one facet of the challenge that tweens present us in the classroom.

When I first began musing about this book, I knew that I would include the anecdote in the introduction about Natalie and her naked reading. I meant the term *naked reading* to reflect the abandoned and oblivious joy Natalie (and others) derive from the reading experience. The anecdote posits the question that I thought was at the heart of this book: Why do some kids become so fully immersed in reading that time and place (and clothing) are unimportant while others elect not to be members of what Frank Smith calls "the literacy club"? It seems essential not only to examine why some kids love reading and others do not but also to demystify some of the terminology and get down to the bare bones to examine what works and what does not. So, before we launch into a full-blown discussion of tweens and reading, let's pause for some important observations and perhaps a few definitions.

Kylene Beers (1990), in her ground-breaking research into the lives of aliterate students, drew one conclusion that continues to impress itself onto my mind every time I talk about books and readers. Beers asserts that there is no one "template" for aliterates, kids who know how to read but elect not to join in. Instead, Beers points to several different templates for these nonreaders. Some elect not to read because their life is simply too hectic; others do not read because they cannot locate books that interest them; still others do not read because reading poses problems for them. I think that the same is true for tween readers: there is no one template that fits all. Tweens are as varied as the music they program into their I-Pods, the clothes they buy from Old Navy and The Gap, and the books they select for their own personal reading. Some tweens are mature and savvy; others are less so. You have only to look at the discussion of Brad and Andrew that opens this chapter to see how wide-ranging readers can be at this age and stage of development. Having said that, there are some generalities that can help us as educators to work more successfully with tweens. Some basic information about tweens and how they develop, including how they develop into readers, can inform classroom practices and assist us as we strive to create tweens who become lifetime readers.

Tweens and Teens: Some Clarification

Before we set off on our journey, it might be wise to stop for a moment and make sure of our directions by setting some definitions. What do I mean by the term *tween*? This definition has caused considerable debate. When *Time* magazine used this term several years ago, it was to refer to kids between the ages of ten and twelve; those individuals who were no longer children but not quite teens. That definition, in my opinion, is a cultural one that sets too many limitations. Given that narrow a definition, this book would focus on students in grades 4, 5, and 6 only. While students in intermediate grades are certainly part and parcel of the tween group, I choose to extend the age limitation to include students in grades 7 and 8. In terms of chronological age, these students are teens and not tweens. In many ways, though, seventh and eighth graders are still "between." They are between playing with Barbies and wanting to look like Barbie; they are between children's books and young adult novels as reading fare; they are between dependence on parents and educators and self-direction in their lives and their learning.

So for the purpose of this book, I include a discussion of the tween population as well as those younger teens, focusing on students in grades 4 through 8; roughly, kids age ten through fourteen. In many ways, this is the group that tends to fall through the cracks. Reading First and No Child Left Behind directed the attention of educators to kids in early and primary grades. By third grade, all students were to be reading on level and, at least as far as the legislation is concerned, kids are to remain on level for the remainder of their school years. By high school, there are many programs in place to ensure that more and more of our students graduate. But what about those students between fourth grade and ninth grade? The trouble is, some of the kids in grades 4 through 8 either did not read this legislation or just do not care what they are expected to be able to do. More and more teachers are remarking that, beginning in fourth grade, kids are turning away from reading, that the amount of reading for pleasure is dropping during these tween years. Data from the NAEP bear out the teachers' reports. Though headlines from the latest NAEP reports tout gains in reading from previous tests, a closer scrutiny of the scores suggests there are still many hurdles remaining for educators.

For example, the NAEP results for fourth grade indicate that more than 30 percent of students score below Basic and only about 30 percent score above Proficient in reading (NAEP 2005). Yes, students are making gains in basic comprehension skills; however, the more proficient skills of literary appreciation and analysis still elude many readers in intermediate and middle school. By eighth grade, the statistics are not much better: at least 25 percent of students score below Basic and approximately 30 percent score Proficient (NAEP 2005). Perhaps more disturbing is the fact that reading done outside school—what we would typically label reading for pleasure—continues to drop from grades 4 through 8. Students are electing *not* to read more often. We will continue to explore the reasons for this decline, but the fact that it exists is cause for concern on the part of teachers, librarians, parents, and administrators.

Tween Psychology: It's Not a Tween-Age Wasteland

Ann Hurlbert (2003) remarked in an article that this time in the life of our children is all about *transience*. As students grow and move from elementary to intermediate and on to middle school, there are tons of transitions they must make. Remember how traumatic it was to move from one school building to another? I still remember those poor sixth graders in my former middle school on the first day of school. The sixth grade classrooms were at the opposite end of the hall from our eighth-grade classrooms, but even from afar, it was obvious on that first day that the simple things eighth graders took for granted presented enormous challenges for the sixth graders down the hall. Finding classrooms was traumatic enough, but knowing you had to move from classroom to classroom every time a bell rang was positively painful for these students, never mind negotiating lockers and locker combinations! Eighth graders found these harrowing situations downright comedic in retrospect. But each year the same upsetting scenarios played out in the hallways at the opening of school. More distressing are the bigger transitions that occur as students move through the grades. The transitions we are talking about here are physical, emotional/mental/psychological, and social/cultural. Each transition brings with it its own unique set of factors.

Physical Transitions

During the tween years, kids are transitioning from their childlike bodies to bodies that are more adultlike; however, that transition does not happen in one smooth step. Tweens do not go to bed one night as kids and wake up the next morning in their more adult bodies. Instead, this transition is gradual and, for many tweens, painfully slow. As the hormones that mark the onset of puberty begin to be released, tweens undergo many physical changes, most notably the appearance of primary and secondary sexual characteristics. Babette Cole, in *Hair in Funny Places,* relates this time in truly funny terms as Mr. and Mrs. Hormone awaken and begin to trample through the system of the hapless young girl on the verge of puberty. To the tween, however, be assured there is little to laugh about. It is a matter of either too little, too late or too much, too soon.

Since tweens begin to experience the onset of puberty at different rates, there is no definitive time line. When Corrie my middle grandchild was in fifth grade, her body was already undergoing tremendous changes, whereas her sister Natalie was in seventh grade before these same changes occurred. The same concern that sends new parents running to the Doctor Spock child-care handbook is present during this time in the lives of tweens. Only in this situation, it is the tween who is frantically searching for a handbook, something to help as he or she navigates the troubled waters of tweendom, something that reassures him or her that he or she is "normal" and will survive.

Physical changes include not only the onset of sexual characteristics, but can also include physical growth. Boys and girls grow taller. Hands and feet grow bigger. Shoes are outgrown before they are worn out. Pants seems to shrink with each washing as legs grow and tweens get taller. Just recently, Natalie spent a considerable amount of time ironing some pants she wanted to wear only to discover the next morning that she could not even button the waistband. Her sister, two years older, is being left in the dust as Natalie towers upward. Walk into any classroom in fifth or sixth grade and you will see an amazing array of heights, weights, and body types. And the fact that others are in the same boat does little to comfort kids during this difficult time of transition. Judy Blume understood this transition and its effect on kids several decades ago. Her classic *Are You There, God? It's Me, Margaret* deals with Margaret's concern about ever being able to fill her bra, get her period, and gain membership in adulthood. *Blubber* and *Deenie* continue to examine the trials and tribulations of moving into puberty and adolescence.

Emotional/Mental/Psychological Transitions

Physical changes, while more obvious, are not the only ones occurring during tween years. Anyone who works with this group understands that there is much going on beneath the surface. How students process information, how they relate to one another, and how they deal with situations all begin to develop and change.

The emotional maturity of students is in a constant state of flux. Some of this is due to hormonal changes. Naturally calm, level-headed kids suddenly seem to be on the verge of emotional outbursts. Tears flow more freely for some; others have a difficult time controlling anger and frustration. For Corrie, this was a time that challenged how she interacted with her younger sister and her peers at school. Her natural inclination was to literally lash out when truly frustrated by the teasing of others. Corrie had to learn how to contain her impulses. It was a learning curve that took some time to take hold. Natalie now reports the same reactions when she complains that her less mature classmates and pals are quick to pinch and poke. Imperiously, she informs us that her friends no longer hurt her; she has grown impervious to their physical means of dealing with their emotions. The fact is, there is also a tremendous range of emotional development within this group. Some kids in fourth grade are mature; some eighth graders are immature. Life experiences, the culture of the home, and other factors account in part for this range.

It has been my experience that books can play a role in the emotional development of this group. As readers dive into a variety of books, they see people solving problems, dealing with obstacles, and negotiating difficult situations. Each of these characters in search of solutions for their problems becomes, in essence, a role model for readers. Should they ignore the problems and hope they go away on their own as Joel does at first in Marion Dane Bauer's *On My Honor*? Does it help to avoid talking about a painful loss as Jack does in *Love That Dog* by Sharon Creech? Or is it better to confront the problem head on in a blog as Raisin does in *The Secret Blog Of Raisin Rodriguez* by Judy Goldschmidt or find someone in whom to confide like the title character in *Rodzina* by Karen Cushman? Since there is a range of emotional development, we need to find a range of books that meet kids where they are and help them make the important transitions from childhood to adulthood.

An article in *Newsweek* magazine (Kantrowitz and Springen 2005) points to the Five Cs as being essential for the psychological development of tweens and teens. The Five Cs are: competence, confidence, connection, character, and caring. These aspects of psychological growth are also part and parcel of the books available for our students. Figure 1.1 lists some titles that focus on each of the Five Cs. Annotations for all the following titles may be found in the appendix.

Figure 1.1—Books That Focus on the Five Cs

COMPETENCE
Chasing Vermeer by Blue Balliett
Love That Dog by Sharon Creech
Drawing Lessons by Tracy Mack
Matchit by Martha Moore
Sparks by Graham McNamee

CONFIDENCE
Backwater by Joan Bauer
The Tale Of Despereaux by Kate Dicamillo
The Misfits by James Howe
The Truth About Sparrows by Marian Hale
Girlwonder by Holly Hartman

CONNECTION
The Colors of Freedom by Janet Bode
911: The Book Of Help Edited by Michael Cart
Getting Near To Baby by Audrey Couloumbis
Ida B by Katherine Hannigan
Olive's Ocean by Kevin Henkes

CHARACTER
Messenger by Lois Lowry
Stand Tall by Joan Bauer
The Rag and Bone Shop by Robert Cormier
Mississippi Trial, 1955 by Chris Crowe
The River Between Us by Richard Peck

Figure 1.1—Books That Focus on the Five Cs (cont.)

CARING
Sisterhood of the Traveling Pants by Ann Brashares
Al Capone Does My Shirts by Gennifer Choldenko
Rodzina by Karen Cushman
Hoot by Carl Hiaasen
When Zachary Beaver Came to Town by Kimberly Willis Holt

A huge mental or intellectual transition is also occurring at this time, compounding the slings and arrows of tweendom and adolescence. The transition most worthy of note for those of us who work with these students is that from concrete to more abstract learning. Remember, there is no one template for this age. Kids move from concrete to abstract sometime during the ages of ten and fourteen. So some fourth graders find algebraic concepts and literary questions about symbolism and theme just fine while for some eighth graders who have still not made the transition, these same questions elicit that dreaded shrug followed by the "dunno" response. Even more frustrating from our perspective is that students in the same class can be in very different places along the continuum of change from concrete to abstract. How can we deal with this range and still leave no child behind? Chapters 2 and 3 offer concrete suggestions.

Finally, there are changes in the psychological development of kids during these crucial years. Students move away from an "it's not fair" attitude and begin to think more about what is good for the whole—developing a sense of social justice, if you will. In Kohlberg's terminology, students move from preconventional to conventional means of making decisions. No longer is it a matter of reward and punishment; now it is a matter of following rules and procedures.

Social/Cultural Development

Social and cultural development is difficult to separate from the preceding discussion. Moral, mental, and emotional development affect social and cultural changes greatly. At this stage in their development, tweens are beginning to forge new relationships within society. They are no longer "little kids to be seen and not heard." As a matter of fact, they are the target population for ad execs and companies looking to create brand loyalty. These kids are heard. They are making their way slowly, negotiating some of the early roads into adolescence and adulthood. For example, many tweens already possess a sense of what is right and fair, at least in terms of how they see the world and what is happening in it. Think of the response of our tweens at the time of the events of 9-11. Think of all the kids who dug into piggy banks to send money to the tsunami and Katrina relief funds. One brother and sister, ages twelve and fourteen, started Operation Backpack to send backpacks loaded with school supplies to evacuees from New Orleans who had to face going to school in a new community. They managed in one week to send out more than 5,000 backpacks. This is social growth at its finest. Kids have already developed some sense of caring and character, two of the important Cs noted above.

In some ways, books help develop this sense of empathy when readers identify with the main character and her or his struggles. Kathi Appelt's *My Father's Summers: A Daughter's Memoir* is a story that can create strong empathetic bonds as kids read about what life was like after Kathi's parents divorced and her father remarried. A piece from this book entitled "Steps" talks about all the steps in her new relationship. She now has a stepmother and stepsisters; steps separate her from her father; she needs to watch her step when talking to one parent about the other. Any child who has been in the center of a less-than-amicable divorce knows about these cautious and fractious steps. Even Bruce Coville's hilarious *My Teacher Is an Alien* can strike a responsive chord with readers who are certain that their teachers must be from another planet! Tweens who have read *Getting Away with Murder: The True Story of the Emmett Till Case* by Chris Crowe respond with horror at what they can already perceive as the injustice that existed long after the Emancipation Proclamation.

From a cultural perspective, too, the tween years are a transitional time. Examine, for instance, the cultural traditions that occur during these years. In many religions, tweens are beginning to be welcomed as full members of the various faith communities. Celebrations mark the movement from single-digit to double-digit birthdays. Kids get too old to go trick-or-treating at Halloween, but remain too young for other things. Many of you reading may recall the fateful year that you were finally invited to come and sit at the adult table at Thanksgiving dinners (or perhaps some of you are still waiting for that transition?). New freedoms and new responsibilities are all part of the transition from childhood to young adulthood.

Development as Readers

I do not remember a time when I was not a reader. I have early memories of sharing a seat in my Pop-Pop's wheelchair and reading books together. I remember "borrowing" my mother's copies of *True Confessions* to read under the cover of darkness. My trips to the library to use my own library card to check out books were better than our trips out to eat at Big Boy. Christmas gifts always included a set of whatever series I was reading at the time.

Now, I watch as my college freshman, Cali, winces at the prospect of having to take an English class because it will mean reading. The other evening at dinner we talked about how to deal with Accelerated Reader (AR) at school. Accelerated Reader (AR) is one of a handful of programs advertised to increase reading as well as scores on reading tests. Basically, in an AR approach, after students read books from the approved lists, they are directed to take a multiple choice test that covers the content of the books. Students receive points for scoring well on these tests, and many schools provide incentives for students that reward their reading. AR and other programs promise increased reading and test scores, but the programs have some major flaws from a pedagogical perspective. For example, the programs assert that the external motivation of points and incentives earned for reading will become intrinsic motivation after a period of time. There is no replicable evidence to suggest that is true. Furthermore, students are forced to read books within a range of reading levels. Students who score well on the quizzes are then guided to books of higher readability and, in some instances, their reading goals are also raised. The concept behind this "pushing" is that it continually challenges students to read more and to read more complex books so that they demonstrate growth in reading. From my perspective though, this continual adjustment is counterproductive. The reward for reading and for scoring well on the quizzes is to be forced to read more and more difficult books. Hence, the dinner table topic du jour. Corrie was telling Natalie about how AR would change in junior high. We discussed not getting more points than those required as reading goals for each grading period and not doing so well on the tests that reading levels would be raised. How sad to think that we are advising our kids *not* to do well with these canned programs. How sad to think that Corrie and Natalie might one day *not* love to read as much as they do now. And the saddest thing of all, for me, is the realization that their growth and development as readers is placed at risk by tests over reading, even reading for pleasure.

How should readers develop during these tween years? If we examine the stages of development in the creation of lifetime readers, we know that certain books and experiences are crucial to helping students grow to be adult readers. Once again, there is no one template for tweens, nor will all our students progress in lockstep through the various stages of developing a love of reading. Instead, we need to offer books and experiences that will allow our students to make their own progress through the stages of *unconscious delight, reading autobiographically, reading for vicarious experiences, reading for philosophical speculation,* and *reading for aesthetic experience.* These stages of development have been identified, discussed, and defined by several experts in the field including G. Robert Carlsen (1988), Ken Donelson (1996), and Aileen Pace Nilsen, and Margaret Early. The work of these educators provides us direction as we choose books and activities to share with our students so that they might become lifetime readers.

Lifetime readers elect to read even when they do not *have* to read. They differ from schooltime and worktime readers in this way. Lifetime readers are a small segment of our adult population, as the following statistics demonstrate.

First, 90 percent of all the books purchased in the United States each year are purchased by as little as 10 percent of the population. Are you doing your part? I know I am. I still spend hundreds if not thousands of dollars each year buying books and audiobooks. At one time, when independent bookstores were still around, I was known by my first name. The salespeople set books aside for me to review when I came in for a visit. Sadly, the mega-bookstores are not quite like this, but I still feel the pull to go into a Border's Bookstore or a Barnes & Noble when I visit a new town or mall.

The second statistic is even more disturbing. The average American adult reads fewer than three books per year for pleasure. And America leads the world in the amount of pleasure reading done annually. This is not what I would label a first-place finish to be proud of. I read more along the lines of three books a week for pleasure, and most of my friends report that they read at least three books a month. How in the world can we encourage our kids to become a "nation of readers" when we are, instead, a nation of television watchers? If our children do not see us as readers, what unspoken message does that transmit to them about the value of reading in the adult world outside of school?

Finally, more than 75 percent of teens graduating from high school indicate that they will never read another book again. Think of this: in a typical graduating class, four out of five students who cross the stage to accept their diploma are rejoicing because they never have to read again! An article in the *Washington Post* (Strauss 2005) examines the odds stacked against reading for pleasure due to the increased emphasis placed on standardized testing and a required canon of literature, especially at the secondary level (grades 6–12). It is an indictment of a system that manages to make certain kids read while in school but does precious little to ensure that reading continues past formal education. What can we do in our classrooms to help create lifetime readers? We can provide our students with the following reading experiences as we encourage them through the stages of development in becoming lifelong lovers of books and reading.

Unconscious Delight

Unconscious delight is the time in our reading lives when the real world drops away and we become lost in a book. I must confess that I can fall into unconscious delight even at 35,000 feet in an airplane. Books draw me right into their story until I am no longer sitting in a cramped seat eating my bag of peanuts, but am transported to the bedroom of a young girl who has vowed to give up being Jewish for Lent (*Confessions of a Closet Catholic* by Sarah Darer Littman) or to a magic kingdom created by Jess and Leslie in the woods near their homes (*Bridge to Terabithia* by Katherine Paterson) or to Hogwarts School (Harry Potter series by J. K. Rowling), or even to Alcatraz Island at a time when families lived right next door to the infamous prison (*Al Capone Does My Shirts* by Gennifer Choldenko).

We enter these worlds of books, become lost in the journeys of the characters, and emerge at the end changed in some way. The ability of a book to transport a reader is magical. Fortunately, providing those books to readers does not require a wand or a spell; it all boils down to finding books that speak to the reader. Chapters 2 and 3 provide some guidance for selecting those books for our students, and the appendix gives teachers a list of more than one hundred books, including the foregoing titles, that will transport readers to unconscious delight.

Reading Autobiographically

At some point in our reading, we want to meet characters who share some characteristics of our own lives. We want to see someone like us. As a child of divorce growing up in the fifties and sixties, there were no books that reflected my family. Most of the families in the books I read had two parents and two kids. I think I became a fan of the Nancy Drew series of books in part because Nancy lived in a single-parent family due to the death of her mother. There were no books like *Dear Mr. Henshaw* by Beverly Cleary, in which Leigh Botts struggles with the divorce of his parents and a largely absent father. When I read *Unfinished Portrait of Jessica* by Richard Peck, I felt a familiar pang of recognition as Jessica deals with conflicting emotions about her parents' divorce. Does her loyalty lie with her mother? Can she feel anything but resentment toward her father?

Think of the challenges that reading autobiographically can present to us as we attempt to find books that mirror the lives of our students. We search for stories in which the main character is Asian, mixed race, Jewish, Muslim, overweight, learning disabled, adopted, living in a shelter, physically challenged, small for her or his age, large for her or his age, or falling in love with his or her teacher. Reading autobiographically, then, means finding oneself in a story. It ultimately means that our challenge as educators is to help all our students see their lives reflected within the pages of a book. The diversity of a collection, whether in a classroom or school library, is essential if students are to be able to read autobiographically.

Vicarious Experience

For some tweens and teens, reading about characters like themselves is the last thing they want to do. As the oldest child in a family of four sisters, I particularly enjoyed reading Nancy Drew books because: (1) Nancy was an only child and did not have to share anything; and (2) Nancy did not have an adult directing her every action. Her mother was dead, and her father was largely too busy with his own job. For me, reading for vicarious experiences was of paramount importance.

While I enjoyed the carefree adventures of Nancy Drew, Corrie lives vicariously through Harry Potter, Darren Shan, and the Baudelaire orphans. Natalie, too, enjoys the exploits of Harry and the Baudelaire children, in addition to the mages and wizards and magical beings of the worlds created by Tamora Pierce and C. S. Lewis. The reason for their appeal is still the same: when reading about Hogwarts and Harry and his pals, Corrie and Natalie and millions of other readers imagine what it might be like to travel to exotic worlds and have splendid adventures without parents and pesky peers and limitations.

At this stage, we can expand the reader's world by breaking down barriers and exploring other cultures, other places, and other times. So, while fantasy and science fiction are popular genres during this phase of reading development, there is also room for historical fiction and nonfiction that will help readers discover what connects us as humans despite our different races, religions, and so on.

Philosophical Speculation

Sometimes we read to wrestle with the larger questions of life. Who am I? Why am I the way that I am? What am I supposed to do with my life? What do I want to be when I grow up? Why is the world the way it is? Granted, these questions are not within the purview solely of tweens and teens; they are questions many of us grapple with throughout our lives. When kids read, they can begin to see how other characters wrestle with these same questions. Within the safe confines of a book, it is a simpler matter to ask and attempt to answer these questions.

This leads me to an important observation. Many times I am asked to talk about books in terms of appropriate audience. As I discuss here and in *Making the Match: The Right Book for the Right Reader at the Right Time, Grades 4–12* (Lesesne 2003), I take into account the development of the reader intellectually, emotionally, socially, and culturally. The age of the main character and other elements can also be useful when determining potential audiences; however, I am not one who seeks to "protect" kids from subjects in books because they might be intense. Instead, I would rather my own kids read books in which the main characters are battling drugs, deciding about entering into a sexual relationship, straining against the rules of their parents, and other situations. Unlike real life, it is possible to put a book down if it gets too scary. And do not underestimate tweens and teens: they are fiercely courageous, especially when their books offer a safe place to consider tough questions.

Here is one of my favorite personal anecdotes about readers who want to explore subjects within a book. Last year, *Luna*, by Julie Anne Peters, was one of the finalists for the National Book Award. Peters is one of the brilliant new voices in YA literature, so I had brought the book home to read. It sat on a table in the living room, part of an ever-growing stack that resides beside my TV chair. Whenever I have a moment, I want to have a book handy, so there are always a few books there. Natalie and Corrie take books from that stack as well. Natalie picked up *Luna*, read the blurb on the inside cover, and asked if she could read it. *Luna* is the bittersweet story of a young man who knows he is transgendered from an early age. I told Natalie that I had to read the book first, not because I wanted to make sure it was okay for her to read, but because I wanted to scan the cover and add an annotation to my best YA list of the year if I liked the book. When I finished my reading, I handed her the book. She looked me straight in the eye and told me she had one question she needed to ask before she read the book. I steeled myself for the talk about sexuality and transgendered youth. Instead, she asked, "Does it end happily?" At the tender age of eleven, Natalie already knew that characters who were different did not always live happily ever after.

So I do very little at home in terms of limiting my kids' access to books, particularly children's and YA books. I would rather Cali, Corrie, and Natalie read something challenging and then come to me with questions so we can tackle the issue together. That said, as a former classroom teacher, I had to exercise some caution about the books I placed on the open shelves of my class. The books listed in the appendix all have suggested audiences noted. These suggestions are based on the development of tweens and teens. Books that help readers deal with philosophical subjects are another important piece in the development of readers.

Aesthetic Experience

In the fourth stage of reading development, we read for the sheer beauty and pleasure that reading can bring. This stage includes books that we read more than once. I think of the hundreds of kids I know who have read Harry Potter over and over again. As they wait for the next book in the series to be published, they reread the ones before it.

Books read for aesthetic experience also contain passages, characters, scenes, and or sentences that make us pause as readers—usually because we connect with the books in some specific way. *Love You Forever* by Robert Munsch is one of those books that, while written for children, has much more of an adult message and appeal. A new mother cradles her infant and sings about her eternal love as the book opens. As the boy grows older, the mother continues to cradle him in her arms late at night, all the while crooning her song about loving her child forever. Eventually, the mother grows too old and sick to cradle her son so he scoops her into his arms and sings a song about his eternal love. Then, he returns home to his new baby daughter and continues the tradition begun by his mother. Kids do not find this book nearly as touching as do mothers. I gave this book to my mother years ago on Mother's Day and watched her expression shift from confusion (why are you giving me a children's book for Mother's Day?) to incredibly heartfelt love of the story (we must get copies for all your sisters). This is a book that touches a resonant chord within the reader.

There are many books that can elicit that same response from younger readers. I recall Cali crying as she read *No Pretty Pictures: A Child of War* by Anita Lobel. Corrie nearly choked with laughter as she read the opening pages of *The Watsons Go to Birmingham, 1963* by Christopher Paul Curtis. Natalie so loved the Narnia books by C. S. Lewis that she wanted to write him an e-mail.

I have many favorite books that I share with students as I go into schools each year to conduct booktalks. They are the books that evoke laughter or tears, books that touch the lives of the students I talk to, books that can leave readers with more questions than answers. The appendix contains many other titles of books that may provide an aesthetic experience for your students.

Knowing a bit about the physical, mental, and emotional needs of tweens is only a starting point. Now that we have a working definition of the tween, it is important to explore the world of books and other reading material that is developmentally appropriate for this population. We need to examine what it is that will appeal to tweens and help motivate them to a lifetime of reading. So it is time to turn our attention to what it is that tweens want and need in books as well as what we as educators can do to follow up on their reading. Chapter 2 explores the results of some important research that can and should inform our work with our students.

chapter 2

Books Tweens Prefer to Read: Some Suggestions from the Kids Themselves

Quick Takes: Erin, age twelve

Erin is the quintessential reluctant reader. She will dutifully read assignments for her classes, but she does not elect to read for pleasure. "There are no good books," she proclaims with utter certainty. "All the books we have to read are just boring. Why would I want to take something else home to read? I just don't like to read at all." After watching Erin in her school for several days, though, I began to question her designation as a nonreader. I frequently saw her sitting with some friends and flipping through the pages of Teen People *magazine. When I asked her about what I observed to be reading, she was nonplussed. "We aren't really reading unless we find something about someone on TV. And it's not like I can use this for a book report or anything. So how can this be reading?" Erin's remark is, in some ways, typical of many tweens. They do not consider reading materials other than books to be "real" reading. For some kids, unless it is from a textbook or another assigned book, it is not reading. And if you cannot write a book report about it, it must not count either. In large part, this is because we as educators do not always recognize that reading takes many forms.*

Given the increased presence of graphic novels, manga, and other formats, perhaps as educators we need to redefine what reading is and what it looks like.

Thousands of children's books are published in the United States each year. They have become a billion-dollar industry. In the two years it took for this book to come to press, more than 10,000 books were published, about 3,000 of those for tweens and teens. How do we decide which books we will read, perhaps purchase, and add to the classroom library? In this chapter, we examine the types of books most preferred by tweens and teens.

Sometimes I am asked how I decide which books I will share with groups of students. I admit that in the past there was no particular rhyme or reason for the books I would select for booktalks at local schools. When I did booktalks for kids as a middle school teacher, I had a captive audience and the leisure to come to know each and every student on a more personal level. Now that I am working with older students at the university, I find myself drawn back to the classrooms and to the kids. Now, when I enter a middle school, I am there as a guest speaker, someone to speak to students about books for leisure reading. Now my approach to booktalking is quite different. You need only face hundreds of middle schoolers sitting on the floor of the library to know that you better have some sense of what they will sit still for. The first few sessions I conducted for kids who were not my own students were a trial of sorts, as I tried to come up with some books that would have universal appeal. So I began asking librarians and teachers to jot down which book students actually checked out and read after one of my visits.

For the past fifteen years, I have kept track of the books students in these booktalking sessions prefer. I talk to students as often as I can about their interests and preferences. In addition, I have surveyed thousands of students and teachers in Texas and across the country, and my graduate students have surveyed the students in their schools and libraries. What they all tell me is borne out again and again in the research others are doing. Here, then, in order of ascending popularity, are the five most popular types of literature for students in grades 4 through 8: subliterature; nonfiction; horror, suspense, and the supernatural; humor; and mystery.

Subliterature

I first came across the term *subliterature* as a graduate student in Dick Abrahamson's YA literature course. This umbrella term encompasses some of our students' favorite types of books: comic books, magazines, and series books. This reading material is most often associated with reading for pleasure and/or reading outside of the classroom. If students indicate, however, that they prefer this category of literature, perhaps it should be one of the pit stops we make on our journey. What do these types of materials have in common? Why do students express preference for them? How could we incorporate some of these materials into our classrooms?

The Lure of Comics

Comics are by no means a new genre in the field of literature for children and young adults. Comic books, which began as a compilation of comic strips, have been popular reading material, especially for male readers, for decades. The classics continue to draw, with Superman and Batman and Wonder Woman still pulling fans into stories. They have been joined over the years by the Powerpuff Girls, the Japanese anime influence, the Justice League, Teen Titans, Transgenesis, and even a comic about basketball star LeBron James. A Google™ search will net millions of hits for DC Comics alone. What is the allure of this type of subliterature? A partial answer lies in the fact that the illustrations help to convey the story. They elaborate the few text lines and develop the character and drama or comedy of the story being told. In some ways, comic books take the place of the picture books of our childhood. They tell a story using a few simple words with many illustrations. They are stories of wish fulfillment, where a puny Peter Parker can become Spidey and rescue the damsel in distress. Additionally, this type of reading material is easily accessible in another sense of the word: they are cheap and ubiquitous. Add one final allure: many of the comic book characters of my childhood are now powerful box-office attractions: Batman, Superman, The Hulk, Spider-Man, and Catwoman have all scored big box-office hits with tweens and teens—and some rather grown-up teens too. Some moviegoers are already fans of the characters; others become fans after viewing the movies. Comics, which remain popular among this age group, do not include the graphic novel, a genre that is increasing in popularity, so much so that major publishers are developing graphic novel imprints within their houses. Graphic novels will be discussed in some detail in Chapter 4.

Check-Out Lane Reading for Tweens: Magazines

I cannot get through the check-out lane of the grocery store without one of my kids asking if they can get a magazine to take home, and without perusing the headlines on the cheesy rags myself as I wait. One of my guilty pleasures is reading *People* magazine while waiting in the doctor's or dentist's office. Like comics, magazines have a long publishing tradition and have been preferred reading matter for generations of people. Walk into most school libraries and you will see a wall of periodicals that includes issues of *Teen People, Sports Illustrated, National Geographic, Newsweek, Time, U.S. News and World Report, YM, Thrasher, Vibe,* and others. Some magazines come and go, taking advantage of a trend or fad. Witness the quick appearance and sudden demise of *Rosie.* Magazines with staying power are some of the same periodicals that we read as tweens and teens. Admit it, I was not the only one who swooned when The Monkees appeared on the cover of *Teen Beat* or *Tiger Beat.* I secretly cut out their favorite recipes for cookies and mailed off boxes to their fan-club addresses. For my students in the seventies and eighties, the magazines featuring cover shots of Kirk Cameron or New Kids on the Block or Paula Abdul were popular. The faces have changed, but the formulas remain the same. And that is the allure of magazines: they present readers with a known format and familiar content, issue after issue. Like comics, magazines are readily accessible and affordable. Tweens and teens will plunk down cold, hard cash for an issue of back-to-school fashions or new tricks for the skateboarding crowd faster than they will part with the same amount of cash for the most recent Newbery Award–winning novel.

In February 2005, the following list of magazines was posted to the listserv YALSA-BK. The list is the result of a survey of librarians using the listserv in September 2004. Of course, by now it is possible that some of these magazines have lost their popularity; however, this is a good place to begin. Here are the titles most often mentioned as being favorites:

YM
Seventeen
J-14
Twist
Cosmo Girl
Thrasher
MAD
Game Pro

> (Note: the preceding eight titles were mentioned as most frequently "missing" [code for stolen] from the periodical shelves.) Also popular were the following eighteen magazines:

Shonen Jump
Beat
Transworld Skateboarding
BMX Plus
Dirt Bike
Vibe
Electric Gaming Monthly
Teen People
Transworld Gaming
Rolling Stone
Alternative Press
Nintendo Power
Young Rider
Horse and Rider
Horse Illustrated
The Simpsons
X-Men
all DC and Marvel comics

Series Books and Tweens: Are We Serial Killers?

The love of reading serially is one that develops early in the life of a reader. Reading for unconscious delight is generally the stage where the roots of serial reading lie. For me, it all began with the Bobbsey Twins and continued through Nancy Drew, Cherry Ames, and Sue Barton. In my early years of teaching, the top series for teens and tweens were Sweet Valley High and the Christopher Pike horror novels. About a decade ago, Gary Paulsen introduced two popular series for younger readers with The Worlds of Adventure and the Culpepper series. For my grandchildren, the genesis of serial reading was R. L. Stine's Goosebumps series and now his Dangerous Girls and Nightmare Room series as well. Later, they explored Animorphs and Lemony Snicket. Kids in younger grades are gravitating toward The Magic Treehouse books, Hank Zipser, and The Time Warp Trio series by Jon Scieszka. Who knows what their kids will read serially? The fact is that many kids read serially. Some specialize in one particular series. Natalie reads and rereads Harry Potter and Lemony Snicket because, "you know, you miss stuff the first time you read a book, right, Nana?" She can tell you in which book in the series each event occurs. She knows her series books.

Corrie, on the other hand, is a serial reader of a different sort. She has changed from someone who reads a particular series of books to someone who has a special interest in one particular genre of books. After she found Darren Shan and Amelia Atwater-Rhodes, Corrie went off to locate all the vampire books she could find (no mean feat in a middle school library). She has favorite authors, too, and will read Eoin Colfer even when he moves from his well-known and -loved Artemis Fowl series to other ventures, such as *The Wish List* and *The Supernaturalist*. For both girls, and for all serial readers, the elements present in comic books and magazines are part of the allure for serial reading as well. Readers know what to expect when they read serially. They know how the plot will proceed; they know the characters intimately. They have what reading researchers call a "schema" for each successive book in the series or each book in a particular genre. Reading is almost automatic. It is easy, accessible, and enjoyable.

Nonfiction

As a child, a teen, and even an adult, I had little interest in nonfiction. I still do not run to read the latest how-to book, biography, or informational text. I suspect that one of the reasons for this disdain of nonfiction is that my English classes throughout the years all seemed to target various forms and genres of fiction. I can read poetry, plays, and novels. But at the university there was never a class in nonfiction, nor any courses in how to teach nonfiction.

Even so, for many of our students, nonfiction is a preferred genre. One of the most popular books in our household remains *The Guinness Book of World Records* followed closely by *The Top Ten Of Everything* and *Oh Yuck! The Encyclopedia of Everything Gross*. Libraries have a tough time hanging onto copies of *Guinness* and generally order more than one, knowing how tattered they quickly become. If nonfiction is popular with tweens, the challenge becomes how do we locate good nonfiction to use with our students, especially in classroom settings? Teachers might begin by looking at some of the awards for nonfiction books such as the Orbis Pictus Award from the National Council of Teachers of English. Begun in 1990, the Orbis Pictus Award is given for meritorious achievement in nonfiction for children. The criteria for the Orbis Pictus Award include accuracy of facts, clear organization of text, attractive visual design, and interesting style. Honor winners in 2005 include Phillip Hoose's *The Race to Save the Lord God Bird* and *The Voice That Challenged a Nation: Marian Anderson and the Struggle for Equal Rights* by Russell Freedman. Information about previous winners and the award itself may be found at www.ncte.org/elem/awards/orbispictus/106877.html.

The American Library Association also recognizes nonfiction with the Sibert Medal. Given to the author of the most distinguished contribution to nonfiction for children, the Sibert is awarded annually. The Association for Library Services to Children, the group that also awards the Newbery and other medals, lists winners at the following Web site: www.ala.org/ala/alsc/awardsscholarships/literaryawds/sibertmedal/Sibert_Medal.htm.

Bear in mind that nonfiction encompasses a vast array of subjects. If you look at the titles of the books that have won the Orbis Pictus and Sibert Medal awards you can see biographies of Marian Anderson, Sequoyah, and Walt Whitman along with books about tarantulas, the stock market crash, penguin life, and a multitude of topics. Another good source of nonfiction books, particular those for reluctant readers, is the Quick Picks list from the Young Adult Library Services Association (YALSA) of the American Library Association. Dr. Ernest Drake's *Dragonology, Ripley's Believe It or Not, The Homer Book, Monster Garage*, and books about NASCAR, beauty tricks, and hip-hop handbags are plentiful on these lists that can be found at www.ala.org/ala/yalsa/booklistsawards/quickpicks/quickpicksreluctant.htm.

Horror, Suspense, and the Supernatural

The Mediator, Buffy The Vampire Slayer, Cirque Du Freak, Coraline, Scary Stories to Tell in the Dark, Something Upstairs, In the Forests of the Night, Fear Street, Jade Green: if none of these series or individual titles rings a bell, you have a lot of catching up to do in the area of horror, suspense, and the supernatural. My kids love to go to scary movies and shriek along with the rest of the audience. They love these movies: the scarier the better. I prefer to read the scary stuff because I can always put the book down when it gets too frightening and find something else to do to take my mind off those strange noises in the middle of the night outside the house! What is the appeal of this combination of types of stories? Why do kids gravitate toward them and find them motivating to read?

If we think back to Chapter 1 and the stages of reader development we have the answer to the preceding questions. Unconscious delight, that stage of reading when we can fall into the world of the book, explains part of the allure of this kind of story. Even though these stories deal with supernatural phenomena such as ghosts and creatures of fantasy such as vampires, the stories themselves have foundations in the real world. It is the voice of Darren Shan, a young boy who decides to visit a freak show late one night in an unfamiliar neighborhood, and who tells readers of his attraction to spiders, that lures readers into the macabre story of how Shan becomes part human, part vampire. His voice is real at the outset, and so we enter the world of the story willingly. A willing suspension of disbelief is the term used by poet and author Samuel Taylor Coleridge to describe how we can enter into a realm that does not truly exist. We are brought there by the author, who creates a viable world, one that reflects our own yet with its unique elements. Thus, vampires roam the streets of contemporary New York city; a boy sneaks off into the night lured by the promise of wonders he has never seen before; a girl moves into a new flat complete with eccentric new neighbors and a mysterious locked door.

We also read these genres for vicarious experience. It is not likely we will be afforded the chance to fight demons and vampires, to talk to a boy who lived centuries ago, or to avenge the murder of a young girl. But *In the Forests of the Night, The Vampire's Assistant, Something Upstairs,* and *Jade Green* let us do just that. We can experience what it is like for someone to face incredible obstacles and circumstances.

There is a tendency sometimes to think of this literature as escapist. Perhaps that is part of its appeal. Readers can escape the real world and enter fully into the world of the story. Once there, we are often called upon to deal with real-world circumstances and along the way, may also deal with philosophical questions— another stage in the development of readers. In *Something Upstairs*, we deal with slavery and issues related to that time in our history. Coraline helps us discuss fears of abandonment by parents. And *The Vampire's Assistant* allows us to examine the consequences of impulsive actions. Clearly, horror, suspense, and supernatural literature is popular with our students.

Humor

As an undergraduate student, I found myself working in a neighborhood theater as a stagehand. It was, in all honesty, as close as I would come to the stage, and the ham in me loved the work. My favorite production was *A Thousand Clowns*. At one point in the play, the young protagonist observes to another character, "You missed the funny part!" He is speaking to an adult who does not get the humor in a story. In the case of humor as a genre, though, the line that would be more apropos is from the late Rodney Dangerfield, "I get no respect." Humor, as a genre, tends not to win major book awards. It does not get the respect of the more angst-driven stories; it is viewed by many as a lower art form. However, making anyone laugh, especially someone who is in the throes of puberty, is no easy task. I do more than show respect for writers who imbue their works with humor; I stand in awe. Students feel the same way: they want more funny books. The irony is that, as students get older, their books become more and more serious in nature. "Where are the funny books?" they demand to know. Figure 2.1 lists dozens of humorous novels for your students to enjoy. Many of these titles can be found annotated in the appendix.

Figure 2.1—Books to Tickle Your Funny Bone

Act I, Act II, Act Normal by Martha Weston

Adventures of Super Diaper Baby by Dav Pilkey

All American Girl by Meg Cabot

Angus, Thongs, and Full Frontal Snogging by Louise Rennison

Bucking the Sarge by Christopher Paul Curtis

Bud, not Buddy by Christopher Paul Curtis

Captain Underpants and its sequels by Dav Pilkey

The Cat Ate My Gymsuit by Paula Danziger

Cinderellis and the Glass Hill by Gail Carson Levine

Confessions of a Closet Catholic by Sarah Darer Littman

Cuba 15 by Nancy Osa

Curses, Inc. by Vivian Vande Velde

Death by Eggplant by Susan Heyboer O'Keefe

Ella Minnow Pea by Mark Dunn

Everything on a Waffle by Polly Horvath

Extreme Elvin by Chris Lynch

Flip by David Lubar

Flush by Carl Hiaasen

Green Thumb by Rob Thomas

Harris and Me by Gary Paulsen

Holes by Louis Sachar

Hoot by Carl Hiaasen

Hope Was Here by Joan Bauer

How Angel Peterson Got His Name by Gary Paulsen

I Was a Rat by Philip Pullman

If I Were in Charge the Rules Would be Different by John Proimos

Figure 2.1—Books to Tickle Your Funny Bone (cont.)

Invasion of the Road Weenies by David Lubar
Jack Adrift by Jack Gantos
Jack on the Tracks by Jack Gantos
Jack's Black Book by Jack Gantos
Jack's New Power: Stories from a Caribbean Year by Jack Gantos
Joey Pigza Loses Control by Jack Gantos
Joey Pigza Swallowed the Key by Jack Gantos
Just Disgusting! by Andy Griffiths
The Kid Who Ran for President by Dan Gutman
A Long Way from Chicago by Richard Peck
Maxx Comedy by Gordon Korman
Never Trust a Dead Man by Vivian Vande Velde
No More Dead Dogs by Gordon Korman
Nose Pickers from Outer Space by Gordon Korman
The Princess Diaries books by Meg Cabot
Rules of the Road by Joan Bauer
The Schernoff Discoveries by Gary Paulsen
Sisterhood of the Traveling Pants by Ann Brashares
Sleeping Freshmen Never Lie by David Lubar
Slot Machine by Chris Lynch
Son of the Mob by Gordon Korman
Son of the Mob: Hollywood Hustle by Gordon Korman
Stand Tall by Joan Bauer
Sticks by Joan Bauer
Story Time by Edward Bloor
Tales from the Brothers Grimm and the Sisters Weird by Vivian Vande Velde
Teacher's Funeral by Richard Peck
Technically, It's Not My Fault by John Grandits
There's a Bat in Bunk Five by Paula Danziger
Thwonk by Joan Bauer
United Tates of America by Paula Danziger
Vote for Larry by Janet Tashjian
The Watsons Go to Birmingham, 1963 by Christopher Paul Curtis
What Would Joey Do? by Jack Gantos
The Wish List by Eoin Colfer
A Year Down Yonder by Richard Peck

Mystery

Research finds over and over again that the one genre enjoyed equally by male and female readers is mystery. Since most of us work in settings where our classes have both male and female students, this genre should be one we utilize for whole-class reading sets and develop in our classroom and school library collections. More important, it should be a genre we ourselves read often, especially in intermediate and YA fiction categories. Mystery as a genre, like subliterature, is an umbrella term. Mysteries are as varied as the detectives many of us have come to know and love: Miss Marple, Hercule Poirot, Nancy Drew, Perry Mason, the Hardy Boys, and more recently, Lulu Dark (the title character in *Lulu Dark Can See Through Walls*), and Petra and Calder (from *Chasing Vermeer*). Historical mysteries join crime and detective mysteries and biographies that document the crimes and those who solve them.

What is it about mystery that attracts readers of both genders and from a wide range of ages and abilities? Perhaps a large part of the attraction lies in the mentality adopted when we read mysteries. A mystery is a puzzle waiting to be solved by the reader in tandem with the protagonist of the story. Reading mysteries is, in effect, becoming part of the game, part of the puzzle. As an older teen, I read Ellery Queen, Agatha Christie, and other adult mystery authors. I still turn to mysteries when I am looking for a good adult book to read just for fun, and I love mysteries for tweens because I stand a better chance of solving the mystery before the last page when all is revealed. I think that might be part of the allure for younger readers as well. The mystery is relatively straightforward and red herrings are few, so readers feel empowered as they piece together the mystery and work on the solution along with the protagonist.

One place to find good mysteries to share with our students is the web site for the Mystery Writers of America: www.mysterywriters.org/. From here, you can link to the various categories of winners and nominees for the annual Edgar® Award, which includes Best Juvenile and Best Young Adult. The 2005 nominees and winners are listed in Figure 2.2. Winners are noted in italics.

Figure 2.2—Winners and Nominees for the 2005 Edgar® Award

BEST YOUNG ADULT
Story Time by Edward Bloor (Harcourt Children's Books)
In Darkness, Death by Dorothy and Thomas Hoobler (Philomel Books)
Jude by Kate Morgenroth (Simon & Schuster Children's Publishing)
The Book of Dead Days by Marcus Sedgwick (Wendy Lamb Books)
Missing Abby by Lee Weatherly (David Fickling Books)

BEST JUVENILE
***Chasing Vermeer* by *Blue Balliett* (Scholastic Press)**
Assassin: The Lady Grace Mysteries by Patricia Finney
   (Delacorte Books for Young Readers)
Abduction! by Peg Kehret (Dutton Children's Books)
Looking for Bobowicz by Daniel Pinkwater (HarperCollins Children's Books)
The Unseen by Zilpha Keatley Snyder (Delacorte Books for Young Readers)

At this web site, it is also possible to search for past winners and nominees. Note that there are a handful of authors whose works are nominated on a regular basis: Joan Lowery Nixon, Wendelin Van Draanen, Will Hobbs, Frank Bonham, Jay Bennett, Avi, Willo Davis Roberts, Lois Duncan, Nancy Werlin, and Eve Bunting. As you develop your classroom library collection, works by these authors might become the foundation for the mystery section of the bookshelf.

If we listen to what our students tell us about books, we can more easily find books that can serve the dual purpose of motivating students to read and teaching them about the elements of plot, character development, author voice, and style. Books that are utilitarian are wonderful finds, but the bottom line here is books need to lure readers in and invite them to return. The next stage of our journey discusses how to motivate our students to read.

chapter 3

Motivating Tween Reading: Looking at Results from Surveys and Interviews

Quick Takes: Natalie, age twelve (going on twenty-one)

Natalie is already well on her way to a lifetime of reading. She rifles through my backpack when I come home from the office to see if there are any new books for her. She constantly sneaks books from my stack of reading material because she hates to wait for me to finish a book. If she has a spare moment, she is generally reading. She has set up a reading corner in her closet so she can read while her sister watches TV or listens to music. Even so, I still have some concerns about Nat's future as a reader. She was miffed recently when her teacher told the class they would read The Outsiders *by S. E. Hinton as their first novel. Why was she upset? Well, first the teacher did not have enough copies of the book to send home for kids to read on their own. Instead, they had to read only in class. This is a common situation from my perspective, but now I could see it from her point of view. After I assured her I would buy her a copy of the book, she still seemed upset. "The teacher asks all these questions about the cover and the title and what the book could be about. I just want to read the book. I do not want to analyze [her word] it before I read." Natalie has since changed her opinion of this teacher, and she is now one of her favorites. Why? Because when Natalie returned to school having read* The Outsiders *over the weekend, this wonderful teacher immediately handed her a new book to read that she thought Nat would like.*

Now that we have examined the emotional, psychological, moral and intellectual aspects of this population and the types of books they prefer to read, it is time to move on and discuss what they are looking for in books and what we might do as teachers and librarians to motivate them toward a lifetime of reading. Recent research in the field has provided us with a road map for our journey. First, we look at the activities and strategies students find motivational to them *before* they read. Then, we pay attention to the activities and strategies that might provide continued motivation *after* reading has occurred.

Motivating Students Before They Read

Karen Gibson and Vickey Giles recently surveyed thousands of students from kindergarten through grade 12. Gibson addressed the preferences of students in kindergarten through fifth grade (Gibson 2004) while Giles examined the preferences for students in grades 6 through 12 (Giles 2005). They asked these students to respond to a checklist of activities and strategies that had been identified in journals as motivational activities and strategies for prereading. Students indicated which of these activities and strategies they found motivational on a Likert-type scale. Likert scales typically present a statement to the participant followed by a series of choices ranging from *Definitely Yes* to *Yes* to *Probably* to *No* to *Definitely No* or from *Strongly Agree* to *Agree* to *No Opinion* to *Disagree* to *Strongly Disagree*. Here are two examples of Likert scale type items:

Example One:
Root Statement: *Books make good presents for friends.*
Likert scale choices: Circle One
Strongly Agree   Agree   No Opinion   Disagree   Strongly Disagree

Example Two:
Root Statement: *A teacher reading aloud from a book makes me want to read it too.*
Likert scale choices: Circle One
Definitely Yes   Yes   Don't Know   No   Definitely No

Figures 3.1 and 3.2 present some of the preferred activities and strategies from their surveys. Activities and strategies that appear on both lists are those that appeal to students in both elementary and secondary classrooms. Since we are focusing on students in grades 4 through 8, the activities and strategies appropriate for them would ideally appear on both lists.

Figure 3.1–Favorite Prereading Activities and Strategies for Younger Readers

- Being allowed to choose any book you want to read
- Reading in a comfortable place in your classroom like on the floor, in a bean-bag chair, or in a rocking chair
- Being allowed to buy your own book through a school book fair
- Reading books for a contest
- Having the teacher read aloud in an exciting voice
- Having a classroom library
- Reading books to earn money for a charity
- Having the teacher read a book or chapter a day
- Having the teacher take you to the library
- Having the author come to the school

(Gibson, 2004)

Figure 3.2–Favorite Prereading Activities and Strategies for Older Readers

- Being allowed to choose any book you wanted to read
- Seeing the movie or television production of the book
- Having your teacher bring you to the library regularly
- Having a classroom library with many books on different subjects and reading levels easily available to you
- Having the teacher read aloud a section or chapter from the book
- Being allowed to read books with lots of pictures in them
- Having the teacher read aloud a few interesting pages from a book which you can read for yourself later

---

Figure 3.2–Favorite Prereading Activities and Strategies for Older Readers [cont]

- Having your teachers teach with books written especially for teenagers
- Having a teacher or librarian suggest a book for you based on your interests
- Being able to buy your own books through book clubs or book fairs or a bookshop sponsored by your school

(Giles, 2005)

What do these lists have in common? What conclusions might we draw for the students we are teaching in grades 4 through 8? Three common elements present themselves: hearing a book read aloud; allowing students some choice in selecting books to read; and being able to own books.

The Power of Reading Aloud

Having someone read aloud motivates students across the board, from kindergarten through grade 12. The fact that this activity appears on both lists indicates its cross-age appeal and its appropriateness for tweens.

Whether the teacher reads aloud an entire book or simply entices readers with a few pages or chapters, students continue to find reading aloud a powerful motivational strategy in the classroom. While in many elementary schools, reading aloud is still a cherished tradition in the classroom, I have heard the strategy questioned when used in later grades. If students are to be independent readers by third grade, goes the reasoning, why is it valuable to read aloud beyond those first few years? In 1985, the commission examining reading in the United States stated in its report, *Becoming a Nation of Readers*, that the single most effective activity for building to eventual success in reading was reading aloud (Anderson et al. 1985, p. 23). Jim Trelease and others point out that reading aloud remains one of the most effective strategies for connecting kids to books because: "The more you read, the better you get at it; the better you get at it, the more you like it; and the more you like it, the more you do it. And the more you read, the more you know; and the more you know, the smarter you grow" (Trelease 2005). Other researchers point to the effectiveness of reading aloud to students as well (Krashen 2005; Lesesne 2003; Beers 2003; Carlsen and Sherrill 1988).

Beyond motivation, reading aloud helps to develop other important skills, most notably listening and listening comprehension. Reading aloud can also provide students with a model for fluency. Whether listening to a teacher read aloud or to the audio production of a book, students hear how words are pronounced correctly, phrases are read with fluidity, punctuation marks are used as guideposts, and other nuances of reading fluently are demonstrated. Reading aloud can make dialect accessible, foreign words comprehensible, and different characters separate and distinct. Reading aloud is an important strategy for many different populations of tweens, and especially for ESL students. It can make idiomatic phrases more accessible and certainly aids in pronunciation. Having students follow along while listening can accentuate the sight-to-sound correspondence as well. For students who are dyslexic or who struggle with other reading disabilities, reading aloud can help to circumvent problems. Even students for whom reading is not a struggle occasionally do battle with the lack of time for reading. Reading aloud can provide that time to enjoy books within the classroom.

Audiobooks can be used to supplement, but should never supplant, the reading-aloud experience. There is incredible value in listening to the teacher read aloud in class; it is a more personal experience than listening to an audiobook. Seeing the teacher read, observing the expressions on her or his face, and noticing other nonverbal elements of reading aloud are vital. Having noted the importance of reading aloud in the classroom, however, I would be remiss if I did not include a brief discussion of the role of audiobooks in the process. Audiobooks can supplement and enhance the reading experience in several ways. For instance, books set in foreign countries or featuring dialects are ideal for audio listening. While I do a credible job inside my head while reading the latest Harry Potter book, my British accent does not work when I read aloud—it sounds more like East Texas meets East Hampton. So, as a teacher, I might elect to play a portion of the audio for students to hear the incredible mastery of reader Jim Dale. I could also opt to use the entire audio version of this book in the classroom. Alternately, I would play a chapter or two from *47* by Walter Mosely so that students can hear the dialect of the main characters—slaves from a plantation—who are visited by the mysterious Tall John, a runaway slave from another time and place.

Audiobooks can be used alone simply for listening or they can be paired with the book for listening while following the print. I have been working with tweens and audiobooks for several years. We offer students the option of taking the book, the audio version, or both. Whatever the choice, students report positive responses to audiobooks and have returned for more selections. Audiobooks have also become part of students' commute to and from school and even part of their family carpooling.

The Power of the Freedom to Read

A second element that the two lists share has to do with choice. Students overwhelmingly indicate in each of these studies that having choice in terms of their reading material is something that motivates them to want to read more. This finding confirms research being done by Janet Allen, Kylene Beers, and Nancie Atwell, who advocate some type of choice in reading materials for our students. My own research has suggested this as well. When we ask kids what we can do to make them want to read more, they answer emphatically, "Let me pick my own stuff to read." Even reluctant and struggling readers prefer to select books on their own, even if it is from a narrowed selection of titles.

At Moorhead Junior High School in Conroe Independent School District, a suburb north of Houston, librarian Lois Buckman uses a narrowed selection of books to assist her reluctant middle school students in their search for appropriate and energizing reading matter. Her strategy is to locate a few book carts throughout the library, some of which she designates for student use in research for class assignments, while a few sport labels and signs indicating their contents. Lois alternates the books on these carts over the course of the school year. She might begin with some tried-and-true choices aimed at the types of books students want. New additions to the library might be featured one month; a cart in October is sure to have scary stories; February's cart must have love stories as well as love sucks stories. Lois also separates the Texas reading list books onto carts. Like most states, the Texas Library Association each year develops lists of books for students from age two to grade 12. The Bluebonnet list targets grades 3 through 6; Lone Star books are for grades 6 though 8. So, Lois will pull the books for the current Bluebonnet and Lone Star lists and place them on carts. This ease of access has proven effective in keeping students more connected to books and reading. They can locate the books on their own, an important element in building confidence.

Reading aloud and booktalking are also valuable as students seek new material to read. Booktalking, simply talking about books in order to "sell" them to a reader, can take place in the library or in the classroom. Ideally, of course, the librarian participates in booktalks no matter the location. I hold booktalks randomly. I have been known to wander into a school library, select books from the shelves, and conduct impromptu booktalks. I do the same in bookstores and at conference exhibits (I confess: I am a booktalk junkie—if someone is willing to listen, I am willing to talk). The best booktalks, especially for new readers, use some sort of hook or theme. Here are some themes and hooks that work well with this population.

Books with animals as the main characters. For students who love the animal fantasies of childhood, this theme raises the bar with a bit more sophisticated fare. I might begin with some simple animal stories such as *Shiloh* by Phyllis Reynolds Naylor and build to the complex high-fantasy world of Brian Jacques in his Redwall series.

Bloody books. I build from the least gory to the most gory when I can. *Phineas Gage* by John Fleischman is still a no-fail choice for me when I am booktalking, especially to boys. *Rats* by Paul Zindel is another no-fail grisly book to share.

"What would happen if . . ." books. Many books answer this basic question. What would happen if you discovered that your parents have paid someone to end your life? (*The Grounding of Group Six* by Julian Thompson). What would happen if you were a cheerleader who lost her leg in a car accident? (*Izzy Willy-Nilly* by Cynthia Voigt). What might happen if you survived a plane crash with only a hatchet as equipment? (*Hatchet* by Gary Paulsen). As you can see, the possibilities are endless.

Choice has to extend beyond the confines of the school library and into the classroom, however. As we have seen, kids want to select what they will read. Classroom libraries and regular trips to the school library (also mentioned in the research by Gibson and Giles) help them find the books they are seeking. Developing and maintaining a classroom library can be invaluable for keeping kids connected to books. If students complete the book they are reading, a classroom library offers them immediate access to other selections. But remember, as strong a tool as classroom libraries may be, there is still a need for students to regularly visit the school library. There are thousands of choices in the school library and (usually) a certified school librarian to assist teachers and students in locating information and material. Keith Lance (2004) has studied the effects of having adequate school libraries staffed by certified personnel in numerous states. His conclusion: How well students perform on state assessments is correlated to the strength of the school library and its personnel. In this age of information technology, access to the library is crucial for a number of reasons besides motivating students to read.

The Power of Ownership

A final element the lists have in common has to do with ownership of the books. Book clubs and book fairs are all about ownership and, to some extent, being able to check books out of the classroom and school library is a part of this ownership issue as well. Students in all grades noted that buying books through book clubs or a school-run bookstore would make them want to read more. As a parent, I go through the book orders that come home monthly from the kids' teachers. Natalie still wants to buy *everything* in the order form even after I point out that she either has read the book or actually has a copy of it on her bookshelves. I know when the annual schoolwide book fair is approaching because suddenly both Corrie and Natalie ask to do extra chores to earn money.

My friend Lois and I use funds from several mini-grants to purchase multiple copies of books for the various programs we do with kids. Students are permitted to keep books they check out if they so desire. With these small grants, we are able to replenish the books each year. The Reading Is Fundamental (RIF) organization (www.rif.org/) offers some funding for younger children as well as plenty of information for teachers, including lesson plans and tips on motivating readers. Many school districts, some in partnership with local businesses, offer funding for projects within the schools. Check to see if there are funds available to you for purchasing books for students.

Much of my research with students indicates that those from less affluent circumstances own fewer books. This finding is borne out by the work of my graduate students who work in schools across Texas. Each semester, they survey students in their schools to determine how many books are in the home, how many books students own. In the more affluent suburbs of the major cities, students own their own library of books. The reverse is the case for students who come from less affluent neighborhoods. In these homes, books are scarce and ownership of books is a rarity. Stephen Krashen notes: "children and adolescents from low-income families have very little access to interesting and comprehensible reading material at home, in their neighborhoods, or even at school. It is because of this lack of access to books that these students are the ones who score lowest on tests of reading" (2005).

The question becomes, how else can we boost ownership of books? Using bonus points from book-club orders and the bonus books from the book fair might be one solution for placing books in the hands of those who can't afford them. Reading Is Fundamental programs do this as well. As educators, we need to come up with further ideas for remedying this disparity between kids who have access to books in the home and those who do not. At Moorhead, Lois Buckman and I allow books and audiobooks to be checked out of the school library for more extended lengths of time than the traditional two weeks. In some instances, we encourage students to keep books as long as they like even if it means we do not see the return of these materials and have to replace them each year. These suggestions barely scratch the surface. Do whatever it takes to provide students with ownership of books, especially books they treasure.

After Reading, How Do We Motivate Students?

All right, so now we have implemented strategies and activities that motivate *before* students actually sit down to read. We have whetted their appetite. We have provided them with appropriate and motivational books and reading materials (see Chapter 2). Where do we head next? As educators, we know we have to bring some closure to the reading process. What can we do to assess reading while still motivating kids to want to read more? That is indeed a tricky maneuver. Once again, we turn to the research. Figures 3.3 and 3.4 list activities and strategies that students deemed motivational according to Gibson and Giles.

Figure 3.3–Favorite Postreading Activities and Strategies for Younger Readers

- Seeing a video of the book you read
- Taking a test on the computer to earn points
- Meeting the author
- Doing an art activity
- Designing a book jacket
- Choosing another book to read
- Making a picture to go with the book
- Acting out part of the book

Figure 3.3–Favorite Postreading Activities and Strategies for Younger Readers (cont.)

- Making a puppet show from the book
- Dressing as a character from the book and telling about the story
- Talking to your friends about the book
- Talking to a small group of students about the book

(Gibson 2004)

Figure 3.4–Favorite Postreading Activities and Strategies for Older Readers

---

- Playing reading games with books you have read
- Doing an art activity based on a book you have read, such as a mural, a frieze, a poster, a diorama, a mobile, a collage, a cartoon, or a comic strip
- Taking a test on the computer about the book you have read so you can earn points
- Reading books for a reading contest, with prizes awarded to those who have read a certain number of books
- Sharing books and talking about them with your friends
- Making models of the characters in a story out of clay, soap, wood, or plaster

(Giles 2005)

Once again, examining common elements from these two lists shows us which activities and strategies would be most appropriate for our tweens. One common activity has to do with completing a visual representation of the books read—whether in the form of a diorama, a sculpture, a poster, or some other medium. While assessment activities that involve art tend to remain popular in the early elementary grades, they frequently are replaced with more traditional forms of book reporting by the time students hit intermediate and middle school. Intermediate and middle school students still want to cut and paste and draw and paint. Visual representations from the books they are reading are a good way to develop viewing and representing skills, what we call media literacy. Using these skills to report on books combines the concrete with the abstract, making students think on a higher level while providing the scaffolding they need.

Another common feature of the postreading strategies and activities for students across grade levels is the chance to *talk* with someone about the book they have read. All students prefer to talk to their friends; but younger students will also talk to a small group about the books they have read. Talk is the key factor here. When the sixth Harry Potter book was released in the summer of 2005, hundreds of thousands of readers waited in line to pick up a copy. For educators, online discussion of the book began almost immediately. Folks who had not had the chance to complete the reading of the book pleaded for spoiler space in the postings so that the story would not be revealed. I did not do a count of the actual postings that discussed HP6 but I know they numbered in the hundreds in the week of the book's release. YALSA-BK and ncte-middle are two listservs where book discussions take place on a regular basis. I frequently read a particular book just because it is being hotly debated online.

So we need to provide time in class for students to talk about the books they are reading. This talk could take a formal slant, using Literature Circles or Socratic Circles, or it could be less structured, with time for informal sharing of books. Even now, in my university classes, we end each session with a group sharing of those books we read and either loved or hated or both. The talk is unstructured, but I do provide a model of what I want to see in terms of comments about the book. We have a list of forbidden vague words, such as cute, funny, interesting, and boring, and we focus on why a book made us laugh or cry or wince or scream in frustration. What I witness each time we share books is that students make notes of books they hear about in the sharing, books they want to read when they have the time. Talk can help keep tweens connected to books.

Finally, both groups expressed positive feelings about taking a test on the books they had read. What we are seeing here is, I think, the result of the first group of kids coming through school having all been exposed to canned reading programs, such as Accelerated Reader, that require taking a multiple-choice exam before points can be awarded for reading. For these students, taking a test after reading is as natural as it is for you and me to talk to a friend or colleague about our favorite new books. The overriding elements of postreading activities and strategies students find motivating after they have read have to do with visual and oral media.

As enlightening as it is to examine the common elements of the two lists, it is also valuable to examine where the lists diverge and why there are differences between the responses of the younger and older students. Younger students express an interest in meeting the author of a book as something that would motivate them to read more. They also want to see a video or movie production of the book. For older readers, seeing a movie or video is something that would motivate them prior to reading. This is an interesting difference. Older students want to see the movie and then read the book; for younger readers the reverse is true. Older students also indicate a desire to play reading games about the books they have read. These divergent answers indicate that still other strategies and activities may or may not motivate tweens. We need to survey our own classes to determine whether a particular strategy or activity would be valuable.

A final note about the postreading strategies and activities: students across the grades expressed a *dislike* for most activities involving writing of any sort. Figures 3.5 and 3.6 indicate the least favorite postreading activities and strategies.

Figure 3.5–Least Favorite Postreading Activities and Strategies for Younger Readers

- Writing down feelings about the book
- Writing a new ending for the book
- Writing a make-believe letter from one character to another
- Writing another story about the people from the book
- Writing a summary of the book
- Writing a book report about the book
(Gibson 2004)

Figure 3.6–Least Favorite Postreading Activities and Strategies for Older Readers

- Writing a formal book report on a book
- Writing a biography of one of the characters in the book
- Writing a newspaper story based on what happened in the book
- Writing a make-believe letter from one character in the story to another
- Writing your own story with a plot like the one in the book but with different characters

(Giles 2005)

If students eschew writing as a postreading assessment, what options do we have to hold them accountable for the reading without creating a negative attitude? Chapter 5 outlines a baker's dozen of activities and strategies to address this dilemma.

chapter 4

How Can We Energize Tweens?
T-A-R-G-E-T: Six Ways for Teachers to Reconnect Kids to Books

Quick Takes: Brandon, age nine ("almost ten") and John, age twelve.

"I like reading because it's like a journey into a different world where anything can happen depending on what you are reading. Sometimes, reading is like work because you have to concentrate. If you don't concentrate, you have to read the same sentence two or three times. But reading is also like fun because you don't have to have a pencil in your hand or a paper in front of you. I hate writing." Brandon likes mystery books, action and adventure books, and fantasy books such as Eragon *and* Inkheart. *He enjoys guessing what will happen next in a mystery, especially when he is right! Ask him about what he has read or is reading and be prepared to sit and listen for a while. In many ways, John, who is more than two years his senior, echoes similar sentiments. "I like reading because it gets rid of the stress of a long day," says John. "You can just lay down in bed and read a soothing book. My favorite is Harry Potter because it has magic and mythical creatures. It's filled with action and sorcery, and that makes me feel I'm in a whole new world with no worries." A fifth grader,*

John is already experiencing unconscious delight and vicarious experiences with books, as noted in his writing.

When I entered the classroom for the first time in the 1970s, there really was not much in terms of reading material outside of the omnipresent literature anthology and basal reader. Literature for young adults was still in its nascence with only a handful of authors outstanding in the field. Contemporary literature had not even found a foothold in the classroom. Soon after, YA literature began to grow and develop into its own genre separate from literature for children. Zindel, Hinton, Cormier, and Peck produced brilliant works that spoke to contemporary readers in ways that classical literature could not. Over the next decade or so, educators such as Nancie Atwell and Linda Rief began to refocus our attention on the role of *real* books in the reading and English classroom, and classroom libraries began to appear with more regularity. As teachers, we participated in discussion groups, monitored the individual reading being done by our students in the workshop settings we utilized in our classrooms, and read books alongside our students.

The next decade saw more changes. New voices joined in to produce YA literature that enchanted readers: Paulsen, Crutcher, and Kerr, among others. Literature for YA readers grew stronger and books got into the hands of more readers. At the same time another, competing change was coming, brought about in many cases by a sudden focus on student achievement. The pendulum swung from the workshop back to the "basics." Is it any wonder that the literature for these readers seemed to pale as well?

As the focus of our classrooms shifted from workshop to test preparation, other shifts occurred. Before the emphasis on testing in primary grades began, interest and attitude toward reading didn't begin to flag until seventh or eighth grade. Now, with all the pressures placed on educators and students to achieve incredibly high levels on *one* measurement, I am being asked to deal with reluctant and recalcitrant readers as early as in fourth grade. So what used to work well with intermediate and middle school students has to change. Today, we have to be certain that what we do with our students meets the requirements of the curriculum and supports performance on mandated tests. Anyone care to juggle those balls in the air at the same time? What I want to propose in this chapter is not that we add more to our already full plates, but rather examine how we can reconnect students to books and reading while remaining aware of the demands of the curriculum and the tests.

What can we do to bring these readers back to an appreciation of books and reading? Recall, these are the same kids who entered kindergarten determined to read on the first day. Now, they turn up their noses, groan loud enough to be heard, and generally eschew anything to do with books. We have already looked at some of the root causes of this negativity; now it is time to focus on remedies. After all, predicting or reporting failure is rather like predicting or reporting rain. It's nice to know, but does absolutely nothing to change the situation. So forget about the naysayers and analysts who decry the sad state of reading. Instead, take some positive steps to change attitudes and habits. Let's get back to creating readers.

Think of reenergizing readers as the TARGET, something you are going to try to hit with all your skill. TARGET is the acronym I have chosen to describe the characteristics of a program that can successfully produce newly invigorated readers. TARGET translates into these concepts: Trust, Access, Response, Guidance, Enthusiasm, and Tween-appeal. Let's examine each of these in turn.

Trust

First and foremost, our students need to know that they can trust us when it comes to books. They can trust that we know them well enough *and* we know where they are developmentally. Only then can we successfully recommend books that will excite and motivate them to read. I discuss the development of students in Chapter 1. At the beginning of the school year, it might be a good idea to give students a brief survey to get to know them and their reading habits better. While surveying instruments are available from a variety of sources, I prefer to construct my own— something short that will not fatigue the students or increase the time it will take me to go through them all quickly (and, as a bonus, students will not resent having to fill out one more form for me). Consider giving students a checklist of different genres and formats to see if your classroom (and, for that matter, the school) library meets their expressed interests. Figure 4.1 presents a sample checklist you could administer quickly.

I suggest beginning with this quick and easy checklist and then moving on to more elaborate questionnaires and surveys as the year progresses. A second step in this process, then, could be to give students a checklist to assess their attitudes toward books and reading. There are already-published instruments, such as the Estes Scale, that can be used for this step; however, it is also a simple matter to construct one for your classroom's use. Begin with a series of statements about books and reading that are both positive and negative. Sample statements might include:

In my spare time I enjoy reading.

I spend my own money on books.

Reading when I don't have to is a waste of time.

I don't see the need to read outside of school.

Students respond to these statements using a Likert scale, with responses ranging from Strongly Agree to Agree to No Opinion to Disagree to Strongly Disagree. How students respond to each item nets a score from 1 to 5. For example, students who strongly agree to the first two statements that are positive in nature would receive a score of 5 points for each one. Likewise, if they respond with strongly disagree to the second two negatively worded statements, they would also receive 5 points each. On the other hand, students who disagreed with the first two statements and agreed with the second set would receive one point for each of the four statements. Thus, the score of someone with a positive attitude would score a total of 20 points on the four statements; students with less positive attitudes would score lower. Again, you can easily construct such a scale and use it with your students or select from other, already established attitudinal scales.

Once you know more about reading habits, interests, and attitudes, you can begin to plan which books will become part of the classroom library. Note that this kind of evaluation needs to be done for all classes and each year, since students and their interests change over time. When I first began asking my students about the books they preferred to read, romance was the number one response from girls while boys preferred fantasy as their top choice. While fantasy and romance still appear on the final tallies, many girls now read fantasy (though boys have not picked up the romance novel as a favorite), and the popularity of graphic novels, manga, and anime has increased dramatically. A few years ago, I would not have included these categories on the checklist, nor would novels in verse (as distinguished from poetry) have appeared a decade ago. Fads come and go in terms of books. For years, I could not keep enough copies of *Sweet Valley High* on the shelves for my female readers. Ditto *Goosebumps* and *Choose Your Own Adventure* some years later. Now those have been replaced by other series such as the *Lemony Snicket* books.

Figure 4.1–Checklist for Assessing Classroom Library Needs

Place a checkmark in front of the types of books you prefer to read when you have time. I will use this information to help buy new books for our classroom library, so I appreciate your help. If you think of a particular title or author, go ahead and make a note of that, too.

_____ series books (which series?)	_____ nonfiction
_____ poetry	_____ novels in verse
_____ fantasy	_____ science fiction
_____ mystery	_____ suspense and the supernatural
_____ biography and autobiography	_____ humor
_____ comics and comic books	_____ anime and manga
_____ graphic novels	_____ romance
_____ adventure and survival	_____ plays
_____ historical fiction	_____ drawing books
_____ newspapers	_____ magazines
_____ short stories	_____ war
_____ other (please give me some clue here)	

Our students also have to trust that we do not have ulterior motives in recommending books, that we are not attempting to "teach" them something as a result of their reading. One of my favorite children's books is *Everybody Needs a Rock* by Byrd Baylor, with illustrations by Peter Parnall. The narrator talks about the importance of finding your own special rock and the rules you must follow if the rock is to be truly special. I love this book for its simple yet elegant rhythms, for the incredibly awe-inspiring artwork done in earth tones, and for the beautiful allegory it presents me, as a lover of books. Each semester I open classes in children's literature with a read-aloud of this remarkable book and then proceed to explain the allegory I develop from Baylor's rules. The *rock* is the foundation if you will, of a literacy-rich classroom. The rules for finding the perfect rock, for finding the right book, still apply. One of the rules is "always sniff your rock." Kids have a better sense of smell and can tell a rock's origin from sniffing. This rule I liken to those kids who can smell a lesson coming a mile away.

I still remember his name after more than twenty years: Lionel. He handed back a book I had suggested with an expression that only a twelve-year-old can carry off successfully. "Oh," he sneered, "this is one of those books that's supposed to *teach* me something, huh? No thanks." The book was one that talked about becoming a better student. Lionel was struggling in my class, and I innocently thought a book about how to study more effectively might kill two birds with one stone. Not so.

I learned two important lessons. First, do not try to find books that address problems students might be having in class. This process, called bibliotherapy, can have disastrous consequences. After my daughter died a few years ago, well-meaning teachers encouraged my grandchildren, Natalie, Cali, and Corrie, to read books where a main character died. What those kids did not want was to be reminded of their loss. Instead, what they needed was to find some relief from their sadness. We read books with gentle good humor, happy to find a reason to laugh. It has only been recently, some four years after their mother's death, that the girls are reading books like *The Afterlife* by Gary Soto and *The Sledding Hill* by Chris Crutcher.

The second lesson is just as important: as teachers we have to be careful about how much we use books for instructional purposes. It is perfectly fine to study a few short stories, poems, a play, and even a novel as a group in order to learn about the critical attributes of genres, the elements of fiction, or the author's voice and style. If every single book a student reads has to become part of a lesson, however, students will soon learn to dislike books, even those written specifically for them and for pleasure reading. Too many worksheets can also kill. Too many questions turn reading into just another lesson. Donald Graves once remarked that if we grade all the writing our kids are producing we are not doing enough writing with our classes. I think the same is true for books and reading. If we have a follow-up to every book, every read-aloud, every booktalk, we are not doing much to motivate readers. Think about it this way: after you read a book, what do you want to do? Do you sometimes just want to move on to the next book? Certainly you do not rush out to make a diorama to take to your colleagues at school. You probably do not write an official book report. Instead, sometimes it is sufficient to simply move on. Let's think about allowing the same freedom to our students. It will go a long way in developing the trust. Chapter 5 offers some suggestions for assessing the reading of your students.

Finally, students must trust that we will not shy away from tough subjects and challenging books but, rather, provide books that present as much of the truth as possible. For instance, as I am writing this, a novel entitled *Rainbow Party* by Paul Ruditis is making headlines due to its content. Basically, this novel centers on a party given by a group of teens where oral sex will be performed. It is an intense book that is frank in its presentation of sexual scenarios, so frank that most bookstore chains are refusing to carry the book. Now if I were a middle school teacher, I may not have this controversial book as part of my classroom collection. But I would know of the book, would have read it, and would be able to offer an assessment of it to students and parents.

Rainbow Party is an extreme case. It might not be the classic that *Forever* has proven to be. But it does I think indicate how we need to approach books of a controversial nature. As a teacher, *Go Ask Alice* was always a part of my classroom collection. I do not think most of my students were experimenting with drugs, but I do think that most of them were curious about the subject. *Go Ask Alice* afforded them the chance to examine the subject safely within the confines of a book.

Access

What good is motivating students to read if they can't actually get their hands on the books? Students need access to books at all times. Certainly it would be terrific if all parents were like my mom, who made sure I had a public library card and would take me regularly to the library for books. We celebrated Natalie's fifth birthday with a trip to the local library so she could finally get her card and check out books. When Corrie and Natalie are not in school, they love to come to my office and browse the shelves in search of new books to read. They delight in having first dibs on the new Lemony Snicket; they know I will have the new Harry Potter as soon as it is released. However, for some of our students, this is just not reality. So, we need to do what we can to make certain that all our students can access books.

The place to begin is with books in the classroom. Classroom libraries are key to motivating kids to read. The research indicates that even if our classrooms are across the hall from the school library, students are more likely to read if books are in the classroom itself. Building a classroom library is not difficult. Begin by encouraging students to purchase books from book clubs and then use the "bonus points" from their orders to flesh out collections. Haunt garage sales, library sales, and used book stores for great bargains in books. Ask kids to donate books, too. My collection of Sweet Valley High books blossomed in the eighties as readers donated theirs once they finished the reading.

Funding for classroom libraries can come from sources outside of the school. Literacy organizations such as ALAN (the Assembly on Literature for Adolescents of the National Council of Teachers of English) offer grants to teachers for research related to YA literature. I used several small ALAN grants to begin my collection of audiobooks in the late 1990s. Other small grants might come from state English and reading organizations that offer modest research awards each year. Some schools have PTA organizations that support teacher needs through small grants; in other communities there are businesses that offer mini-grant possibilities. To make the funding go even further, purchase books through a vendor or book jobber who offers a deep discount. Bookstores offer educators a 10–15 percent discount. However, jobbers and vendors can double and triple that discount. At the end of many conferences, exhibitors sell the books on display for 50 percent off—or more. Shopping on the last day of the exhibits can be exhilarating (and perhaps dangerous). But a 50 percent discount means twice as many books for the same bucks.

Visits to the school library are also essential. The school library offers much more than we can in the classroom: opportunities for a greater range of materials; access to online computer systems that make locating books and materials easier; and another educator in the form of the librarian, who can help kids find the right book at the right time. The school librarian is one of those incredibly essential folks it behooves you to get to know quickly. I had the good fortune of having the same librarian, Rosemary Smith, for the ten years I taught in Alief Independent School District. Rosemary made it her goal to make her library as welcoming as possible. She knew her book collection and she knew the kids, and she made matches between books and readers constantly. I learned much from her about being a more effective champion of books and reading.

Our class went to the library each and every Friday to listen to Rosemary deliver a new booktalk or two and to have the chance to check out or renew books. Rosemary had a special cart in her office where she would place the newly arrived books that needed to be processed before they were added to the shelves. A few very special people were permitted to take one of those books out and read it before it was officially processed. Basically, Rosemary used this cart as a way to motivate some of the more reluctant readers as well as a reward for kids who lived in the library and for teachers who haunted her door. Now I watch my best friend and colleague, Lois Buckman, lead kids to books in her library using some of those same techniques, plus others truly her own. Lois has added audiobooks to her arsenal in the library and even has an extensive collection of picture books for older students to check out and share with their younger siblings.

Getting books home is another crucial step in motivating readers and keeping them connected to books. My kids have access to tons of books at the house. Not so for many of their peers, though, whose homes contain no books. The problem becomes how to get books into their homes. Lois' idea of having picture books available is one good step in that direction. Audiobooks also help, because the entire family can listen to the same book. Kids in Lois' school reported that they frequently listened to recorded books while going to the grocery store or the mall with their family. Ensuring that students can check books out from the classroom and school libraries is another way to get books into the home—at least on a temporary basis. My former school district, Alief ISD, initiated a program a couple of years ago whereby all the kids in the middle and high schools read the same book. The book was also made available to students' parents to read. This one-book, one-community approach is finding favor across the country. Joan Bauer's *Hope Was Here* has been used statewide. Paul Fleischman's *Seedfolks* was one of the books selected by Alief for their program. Finding books that are of interest to multiple generations of readers is one way to place more books in homes. Figure 4.2 contains a list of some titles that hold appeal across generations.

One final word about access: the book must also be accessible to readers in terms of its contents. I am not talking about reading levels here because there are some inherent flaws in using a scientific formula on what is, in essence, a creative process. That is, reading levels are unreliable. All you have to do to demonstrate this is to look at the reading levels of the following books: *Life of Pi, Fallen Angels, Make Way for Ducklings, Nightjohn,* and *The Adventures Of Huckleberry Finn.* Take a moment and place these books in order from the lowest to the highest reading level, in your estimation. From lowest to highest reading level, the book order is *Nightjohn* (3.8 RL), *Make Way for Ducklings* and *Fallen Angels* (4.2 RL), *The Adventures of Huckleberry Finn* (4.9 RL), and *Life of Pi* (5.7 RL). Interestingly, not one of these books has a reading level beyond sixth grade. Also of note is that few of these titles are developmentally appropriate for most fifth graders. Access, then, is not just readability but takes into account the physical, emotional/mental/psychological, and social/cultural factors discussed in Chapter 1.

Figure 4.2–Intergenerational Books

Al Capone Does My Shirts by Gennifer Choldenko
Becoming Naomi Leon by Pam Muñoz Ryan
Bull Run by Paul Fleischman

Figure 4.2–Intergenerational Books (cont.)

Harry Potter series by J. K. Rowling
Hope Was Here by Joan Bauer
How Angel Peterson Got His Name by Gary Paulsen
Inkheart by Cornelia Funke
Lemony Snicket Series of Unfortunate Events by Daniel Hadler
  (aka Lemony Snicket)
The Liberation of Gabriel King by K. L. Going
Milkweed by Jerry Spinelli
The Outcasts of 19 Schuyler Place by E. L. Konigsburg
Scary Stories to Tell in the Dark by Alvin Schwartz
Sisterhood of the Traveling Pants by Ann Brashares
The Teacher's Funeral by Richard Peck
The Watsons Go to Birmingham, 1963 by Christopher Paul Curtis

---

Response

Although we have touched on the subject of response frequently throughout this book, it is not an overstatement to say that we have to offer our readers many different ways in which to respond to reading. Chapter 5 outlines more than a dozen ideas for students who need to report on their reading. In addition to these ideas, eliciting responses from students requires that we ask them open-ended questions. I have discovered in my undergraduate classes that most students do not understand the concept of open-ended questions. I suspect this is, in part, because they have had little classroom experience with discussions around open-ended questions. Certainly the work of Harvey Daniels in *Literature Circles* (2001) has done much to help teachers and students learn how to discuss books in some depth. *Socratic Circles* by Matt Copeland (2005) takes the concept of literature circles one step further. Both books are invaluable professional resources.

Open-ended generic questions are also good to have on hand for a classroom discussion that truly elicits authentic response. Nancie Atwell's *In The Middle* (1989) and Linda Rief's *Seeking Diversity* (1991) offer ideas for developing these questions. Print out a master list of possible questions and have students keep that list in their notebooks. Not only can such questions elicit a verbal response to reading, they can also serve as a catalyst for writing in response to reading. The following questions will provide a start:

Which of the characters is the most evil, most guilty, most manipulative?

Is there anything in the story that connects with another book you

have read?

Did this book have a "sound track" as you read it?

What does this author do to compel you to continue to read?

Guidance

Taking readers from where they are to where we might like them to be is no easy task. We do owe it to our students, though, to help them grow as readers. There is nothing wrong with reading easy books, nothing wrong with reading to escape, nothing wrong with reading for fun. As a lifetime reader, I occasionally enjoy reading something from the bestseller list rather than rereading one of the classical pieces of literature. One of the guilty pleasures of my life is reading the Captain Underpants series of graphic novels by Dav Pilkey. They are funny, with many different levels and layers of wit, and full of slapstick humor. I do not always read the winners of the Newbery Award nor do I read all the National Book Award nominees or winners. Sometimes I just want to read something light and fun. I think we need to treat students with the same respect for their tastes. While we would never walk up to someone at a local bookstore and tell them to go select a book more "on their level," we sometimes say these very words to our students. So how do we balance respecting kids' tastes with helping them develop into more mature readers? Reading ladders is one solution.

Reading ladders is a concept in which we create a set of related books whose base is centered on students' professed needs and interests, but which provides readers with steps that build from the base. For instance, if students love Captain Underpants (and they do), we can begin with this series as the base of our reading ladder. The trick is to find out why students love the Captain. Is it because the books are funny? If that is the case, our reading ladder is one themed Humor. Figure 4.3 illustrates one possible Humor Ladder with Captain Underpants at the base. It is also likely that readers enjoy this series because of its graphic novel format. That reading ladder might look more like the ladder in Figure 4.4. It is also possible to build a ladder of series books, a ladder of books by Dav Pilkey, or a ladder of skinny books. Building some of these ladders can help us guide readers from book to book, depending on their interests.

While there is nothing wrong with reading favorite books and authors, we do not want our students to be stuck in what I call a "reading rut" where they eschew anything else. So it is always helpful to ask kids about their reading interests and preferences, then try to find other books that would comprise ladders. Reading ladders work because they begin with what students already like and slowly and gradually expand that base to incorporate new reading material.

Figure 4.3—Humor Ladder

Base: Captain Underpants books by Dav Pilkey
Step One: *Disgusting!* By Andy Griffiths
Step Two: *Nose Pickers from Outer Space* by Gordon Korman
Step Three: *Act I, Act II, Act Normal* by Martha Weston
Step Four: *How Angel Peterson Got His Name* by Gary Paulsen
Top Step: *No More Dead Dogs* by Gordon Korman

Figure 4.4—Graphic Novel Ladder

Base: Captain Underpants books by Dav Pilkey
Step One: *The Adventures of Super Diaper Baby* by Dav Pilkey (actually the cover gives credit for the writing of this book to George and Harold, the two protagonists from the Captain Underpants series by Pilkey)
Step Two: *The Wolves in the Wall* by Neil Gaiman
Step Three: Bone by Jeff Smith
Step Four: *Maus* by Art Spiegelmann
Top Step: *The Metamorphosis* by Franz Kafka (graphic novel format)

Enthusiasm

For years, I presented workshops with colleagues Lois Buckman (librarian extraordinaire) and Bob Seney. We spoke at numerous in-services for teachers about books and reading. We called ourselves the B-L-Ts (Bob-Lois-Teri) but someone in an evaluation called us cheerleaders for books. So, one year the B-L-Ts conducted inservices in jeans, sweatshirts, and fluorescent sneakers. We did not need the gimmick; it was simply something that flowed from our natural enthusiasm about the topic we discussed so often. We taught our middle school classrooms with that same enthusiasm. All of us have stories about kids who tried to resist our methods for getting them to read and who failed miserably. We all share those wonderful stories of new readers born in our classes over the years. The B-L-T connection was forged when it became apparent that the three of us shared this remarkable love of books and kids. Our enthusiasm, as it turns out, *was* contagious, not only for our students but for our colleagues as well.

How do we convey this enthusiasm to our students? First of all, we are all models of literacy ourselves. Bob, Lois, and I did not become readers because we were teachers; we were teachers because we were already readers. It was not unusual for our students to come into the classroom and find one of us, feet propped up on a desk, reading a book. And most of the time, that book was recommended by one of our students or one we suspected might be good to share with our classes. We all adopted "Free-Reading Fridays" as part of our regular schedule. We would compact the curriculum to be covered into four days rather than five and then spend Friday enjoying an entire period of free-reading with our kids. We spoke to one another and to our students about the books we were reading and what we thought of them. In short, we modeled what we expected from our classes.

In addition to our literate behaviors, our classrooms were models of literacy. We had shelves loaded with books, books in Tupperware® tubs, books in old crates, books lining the chalk ledge. There was no doubt that when you entered Mr. Seney's room, you were entering the room of someone who loved books. Ms. Buckman's room and mine were adjoining back in the days of open-concept schools. Not having walls in a middle school was such an incredibly, well, stupid thing to do. So Lois and I built walls of books. The books deflected some of the sounds from our classrooms and showed our students that we did more than talk about books; we invested in them as well.

Having books readily available for our students and reading them along with the kids was not sufficient, we discovered, for the more reluctant readers. These students asked us to do more. So we did. We talked about the books we were reading; we talked about the books on the shelves in the classroom. We invited guests to come into the classroom and talk about books. We even arranged for author visits. There was no paucity of booktalking going on in the B-L-Ts classrooms. We not only discussed books with the entire class, we matched books to individual students based on their needs and interests. If I knew Bob had a student who loved the Sweet Valley High series, I made sure I picked up *two* copies of the latest title at the bookstore. Lois would track down the nonfiction drawing books for a group of boys in my class. Bob kept us all up-to-date with the Piers Anthony series of fantasy books that were popular back in the eighties. We booktalked in one another's classes, each of us having special interests in certain kinds of books.

Even today, I am aware of the need to be a model of literacy as I teach students who want to be reading teachers or librarians. I begin each class with booktalks and read-alouds. I blog along with my classes. In short, I demonstrate that what I am saying is actually what I believe and what I do. It is what drives me into schools each year to booktalk to hundreds of kids. And Bob and Lois and I still e-mail and talk to one another about the books we are reading.

Tween-Appeal

The final piece of the TARGET has to do with knowing which books will have tween and teen appeal. Chapter 3 discusses in some detail the types of books that appeal to this population. However, a discussion of other qualities would be instructive. Our students do not select books using genre as a sole criterion. They select books based on other variables. Two of these variables are what I call Kid Variables: age and gender.

While younger and older readers sometimes want different things from books, by the time students are in sixth and seventh grade, they want the same things from books as do their older counterparts. Recently, Natalie went with me to the office to help me shelve and sort books. She always ends up with a sack full of books to take home to read. One of the books she took home from her last visit was called *The Dating Game*. I protested that this book was really a little old for her (I did not tell her she could not read the book), but she informed me that, according to the jacket blurb, this was a book she should read. I was able to translate that into: it is the kind of book her older sister Cali would read, so she should read it as well so she is (in her words) "prepared" for when she begins to date.

Gender is a much more significant factor. Boys and girls look for different qualities in books. Generally, boys prefer to read books in which the main character is male; girls prefer to read stories with female main characters. Of course, there are always exceptions and, it turns out, girls tend to be more flexible in their reading requirements. Girls will read a book about a male main character; the reverse is seldom true. As teachers, we need to assess the books we offer in sets to our students: do we have a mix of male and female main characters? Since a large percentage of teachers and librarians tend to be female, there is some evidence to suggest that boys could be locked out of literacy by having to read "girl" books. YA literature even has a name for a recent trend: chick lit. These books do not attract male readers. Several years ago, author Jon Scieszka began to work on a project entitled Guys Read. The Web site that supports this important initiative, www.guysread.com, contains lots of valuable information and materials for anyone wishing to reach out to the boys in the class.

Other factors fall into the category of Book Variables and include cover, author, title, length, genre, and format. The old saying goes, "Never judge a book by its cover." However, we all do this to some degree, with tweens and teens perhaps even more attracted or repelled by surface qualities such as color, art, illustration, and design. It is not unusual to find different covers for books as tweens and teens go from hard cover to paperback editions. Even new editions of series books undergo facelifts. Witness the new covers of the Lemony Snicket books once the movie with Jim Carrey was set for the theater. The Jack Henry books by Jack Gantos have all had covers recently redesigned. Books that remain in print over a number of years also experience changes in cover art. Do a quick survey in your classroom: select a handful of books and ask students to rank them from 1 to 5 according to the covers only. Which book are they most likely to read? Least likely to read? You will have to hide the titles in order for this survey to work, but it will be an eye-opener. The moral? We owe it to our students to teach them to look deeper than the cover when making selections.

The title plays almost as critical a role as does the cover when it comes to selecting books. *On the Bright Side, I'm Now the Girlfriend of a Sex God* by Louise Rennison is one example of how a catchy title can work to attract readers. *One of Those Hideous Books Where the Mother Dies* by Sonya Sones is certain to pull in readers who might otherwise eschew a novel in verse. Other books that have built-in audience appeal include *When Dad Killed Mom; Boy Kills Man; Dead Girls Don't Write Letters; The Earth, My Butt and Other Big Round Things;*

I Was a Non-Blonde Cheerleader; Confessions of a Closet Catholic; and *Freakonomics.* These are books that benefit from being displayed with covers revealed, not with their spines facing the classroom and would-be readers.

Some students select books based on already developed interests and preferences such as author and genre. I will often talk to students about an author who has a wide range of books in terms of genres, forms, and formats. Gary Paulsen is one of those authors. When he writes from his childhood, his work is largely hilarious: take *How Angel Peterson Got His Name, The Schernoff Discoveries,* and *Harris and Me,* for example. Paulsen also writes lovingly about his appreciation for nature and his love of sledding and sled dogs in *Woodsong, My Life in Dog Years,* and *Dogsong.* Some of his books are historical: *Nightjohn, Soldier's Heart.* Some are nonfiction; some are adventure and survival. Paulsen is a tough author to pigeonhole.

If students are aficionados of a particular genre, I attempt to find books that push the envelope of that genre. Most recently, Walter Mosely's *47* demonstrates how a story can be told from a completely different perspective. Mosely's novel recounts the story of a slave, Number *47,* whose life is changed when a runaway slave named Tall John comes to the plantation. Mosely's skillful combination of history and science fiction/fantasy by using magical realism makes this story memorable.

Finally, length, while not the ultimate criterion for book selection, remains a critical element, especially for reluctant readers. I admit to often selecting a slim book over a fat one. I tend to save the heavy volumes for long plane trips or opt instead to listen to these books in audio format. Skinny books still rule. Here are some skinny books suggested by folks on the YALSA-BK listserv over the past couple of years.

Figure 4.5—Skinny Books: Some Suggestions

Kissing Tennessee and Other Stories from the Stardust Dance by Kathi Appelt
On My Honor by Marion Dane Bauer
The Tiger Rising by Kate DiCamillo
Nightjohn by Gary Paulsen
Bull Run by Paul Fleischman
Sun and Spoon by Kevin Henkes
Olive's Ocean by Kevin Henkes
Witness by Karen Hesse
A Long Way from Chicago by Richard Peck
Miracle's Boys by Jacqueline Woodson

It is important to note that skinny books do not imply easy reading. Most of the preceding choices are tough going. *Witness* is a novel in verse about racism in a small town. *Bull Run* is a novel about the Civil War told from multiple narrators' perspectives. *Kissing Tennessee* is a story collection that forms a narrative. Some titles are historical fiction, such as *A Long Way from Chicago* and *Nightjohn.* So while thin might attract initially, it is not the only criterion for attracting readers.

Reading level is one criterion for book selection that does not appear to have much influence in and of itself when it comes to kids picking books. Unless instructed, most students do not use reading levels to winnow out a choice of book. Although reading levels and lexiles provide useful information to us as teachers, the scientific formulas that produce these numerical indices are not always reliable. We would do better to utilize the criteria above to help us develop a list of books to share with our classes. The final chapter of this book takes a look at what to do now that we have engaged all our students and immersed them in books.

chapter 5

What Can We Do to Follow Up Reading? A Baker's Dozen of Un–Book Report Ideas

None of the information in the foregoing chapters will matter much if we, as teachers, fall into the same old patterns of holding kids accountable for their reading. Accountability is a tricky thing. We need to ensure that kids really *are* reading by recording their progress in some concrete way, yet we know that kids are not so eager to report on their reading. Earlier in the book, we looked at the research conducted by Gibson (2004) and Giles (2005), who surveyed thousands of students about their most favorite and least favorite pre- and postreading activities. This research built on the earlier work of Livaudais (1986). We need to pay attention to what kids tell us are effective accountability and motivation strategies. If we simply hold readers accountable but do nothing to motivate them to read more, then our efforts are counterproductive. So let's examine some ways in which we can kill two birds with one stone: ensure that kids are reading while continuing to motivate them to read.

A few words before we proceed. First, the following ideas are not all-inclusive. There are many brilliant, creative ideas out there in various other publications. Journals, for instance, constantly present us with new ideas for our teacher toolkits. What I offer here are a dozen or so ideas to get you started down the road away from the traditional book report. These are what one teacher recently termed "un–book reports." They allow us as teachers to monitor kids' reading without being so onerous that kids resent the work they do. A second point to take to heart is this: any new approach will work for a short period of time with kids. In research, we call this the Hawthorne Effect. Kids will respond enthusiastically (or at least positively) for a short period of time when something new is presented to them. Then, after a time, even the most creative and engaging activities become rote and, consequently, not motivational. If we ask our students to complete the same set of questions, the same diorama, or the same activity over and over again, they will certainly come to dislike it as much as more traditional forms. The best advice I can offer is this: introduce new forms of the un–book report over the course of the first few weeks of the school year. Do some of the activities as a large group and some with small groups. Offer others as individual activities. Once students are comfortable with the requirements of one type of report, move on to another. After a few months, allow students some choice in terms of how they will respond to their reading. And remember, from time to time even we adults do not want to "do" anything after we read a book. Occasionally, we want to simply walk away from the reading experience and reflect on it ourselves. We need to offer this alternative to our students as well.

Roger Sutton, editor of *The Horn Book,* a review journal for children's and young adult literature, made an essential observation about books, reading, and reflecting in a presentation at the Texas Library Association conference (2005). Reading, he remarked, is primarily a private act. We pick up a book and have a personal transaction with the text. When we are asked to talk about the book or do some report on the reading, we are making a private act public. Think about your own reading. How often, after finishing a truly remarkable book, do you long to run out and get some posterboard and markers or a shoebox in order to make a project out of it? More often than not, we long to talk to someone else about the book we have just completed, especially if it is one that affects us deeply. That was the impetus behind the Oprah Book Club and others that followed. We saw a group of folks sitting around talking about what they liked about the characters, the plot, and so on. There were no quizzes, no essay questions to answer, no "work" to be done; the entire aftermath of reading consisted of talking with others who had read the book. So do not underestimate this simple matter of talking about books as a means of assessing our students' reading.

In the real world of the classroom, teachers must have other tools in their toolkit to hold kids accountable for reading without discouraging them from reading more. Here are some ideas culled from my own experiences working with tweens and teens over the past thirty years. Some are my inventions; others are shamelessly lifted from classrooms and teachers I have visited, from books read, from articles clipped from journals. Take an idea, claim it as your own, imprint it with your own unique particulars, modify it as befits the needs of your kids. In short, make these part of your arsenal. And do not forget to go back and look at the suggestions of Mary Livaudais (1986), Karen Gibson (2004), and Vickey Giles (2005) for other great suggestions for use in the classroom.

Many teachers spend hours planning elaborate lessons for each piece of literature they share with their classes. After fifteen years of teaching middle school I accumulated two large filing cabinets full of these materials (this was before computers made filing cabinets nearly obsolete). After a while, I began to wonder why I kept reinventing the wheel. Surely there must be some activities and strategies that would work well from book to book and poem to poem, and that might even help readers see connections between and among books. I began to put together and use what I now call "template" activities: activities that can move easily from one piece of literature to another.

Template activities not only made my job as a teacher easier, it made my students' lives easier as well. We would spend the first six to eight weeks of school examining various postreading activities together as a class after reading short pieces of literature such as a short story or a poem. Then, when it came time for students to read on their own, they had a "bag of tricks" they could use to report on their reading. The kids became more independent and I did not have to grade hundreds of papers on the same assignment over and over again.

The idea for template activities began to take shape a few years ago when Corrie came home from her first day of fifth grade with a laminated version of the SWBS activity I had heard about at conferences. SWBS stands for Somebody Wanted But So. For this activity, students fold papers into four columns marked S, W, B, and S. They are instructed to complete each column based on their reading. For instance, if I assign Chapter 1 in *The Tale Of Despereaux* by Kate DiCamillo for homework, I ask students, when they arrive in class, to write the name of the main character(s) in the "S" column. In the "W" column, students enter the desire of our young mouse, Despereaux. The "B" column would contain the obstacle that prevents Despereaux from achieving his goal, and the "S" would explain how Despereaux plans to overcome this obstacle. A variation of this activity includes a fifth column, "T" for Then, in which students make predictions about what might happen next.

Corrie's SWBS was on a laminated sheet that was hole-punched and inserted into her English binder. The teacher had asked students to use dry-erase markers or grease pencils on this form in class. I was delighted by this tweak; here was one sheet that could be used again and again either in class or by students as they read independently. Template activities took shape for me with this simple improvement on an already good strategy for kids. The rest of this chapter turns its attention to other template activities students can use independently after they complete reading.

Acrostics

Most teachers are familiar with the acrostic as a poetic form in which the first letter of each line of the poem spells out a message as one reads down the lines. But an acrostic also offers some terrific ways for kids to report on their reading, with tons of variations. My favorite is to ask students to write the title of the book (or the author or the genre, etc.) in a vertical column and to use those letters to tell me something about the book. I ask students to write single words, phrases, or complete sentences. For instance, I might ask kids to write a single adjective (or another part of speech) for each letter, or have each letter form a gerund or participle, a dependent clause, or a simple sentence. You get the drift. This versatile idea combines accountability with additional elements of the curriculum (e.g. grammar studies). It offers plenty of leeway for teachers and for students. Figure 5.1 shows a sample acrostic penned by a fifth grader.

Figure 5.1—Sample Acrostic

Harry Potter is back in book number 6,
A story that will shock many people when they learn who will die.
RAB is one of the mysteries at the end. Who is
    RAB and how will he help Harry and
Ron and Hermione in the final book?
You will have to wait until that book is out to discover whether or
    not Harry

Potter will survive.
Or what else can happen
To Harry and his friends as
They go in search of Snape and Malfoy to
Exact
Revenge

Things We Read from A to Z

A variation of the acrostic activity might be called "Things We Read from A to Z." This activity, from Kylene Beers (2005), presents kids with twelve boxes, each labeled with some of the letters of the alphabet, and asks students—either individually or in groups—to brainstorm words relating to the book they have just read and to place them in the appropriate box. Figure 5.2 presents an example of a partially completed "A to Z" activity. This activity could be modified further to include a comparison and contrast between two books with a related theme, among several books by one author, or within a genre or a series of stories from a short story collection. It could be utilized before students begin reading to activate prior knowledge, or it can be used after reading as one way of assessing comprehension of the text.

Figure 5.2–Harry Potter from A to Z

AB	**CD**	**EF**	**GH**
Azkaban	Dursley		Hermione
Black	Dumbledor		Hogwarts
Beaters			Gryffindor
brooms			Hufflepuff

IJ	**KL**	**MN**	**OP**
	Locket	McGonagall	Prince
	Kreacher	Nearly Headless	Potions class
		Nick	owls

QR	**ST**	**UVW**	**XYZ**
Ron	Snape	Weasley	
Quidditch	Snitch		
	Tom Riddle		

Annotations

Teaching kids how to write summaries is a challenging task. Using the annotation as an alternative to the traditional book report can accomplish two objectives: it serves as a report on reading; and it gives kids practice in writing summaries of longer works. Additionally, an annotation goes beyond a simple summary and asks kids to provide some element of personal response to the book. My approach to using annotations as un–book reports is to provide students with a sheet that explains what an annotation is and what elements comprise it, along with examples of annotations written about books, stories, or poems we have read as a class. One component of the annotation process is writing a bibliographic citation for the book. This one idea helps teach another important skill to students. Students will eventually have to compile bibliographic citations, so why not begin now to give them the tools of the trade? Having students record the bibliographic information for the books they read accomplishes two goals: it gives them hands-on experience that will translate later to research projects and makes it less likely that kids will try to fool us with reports over nonexistent books. Use whatever bibliographic format suits the needs of the classroom. Traditional forms (MLA, APA, etc.) or teacher-prescribed forms work just as well.

Figure 5.3 shows the sheet I provide to students. I laminate and hole-punch this sheet and ask kids to keep it in their English/language arts notebooks or in a folder in the classroom so it is easily accessed. Each part of the annotation serves a distinct purpose in the classroom. The bibliographic citation teaches kids how to prepare bibliographies. The summary can be used to instruct readers about conflict, plot, resolution, and other elements of story. And the response to the book allows teachers insight into how readers felt and thought during the reading. It is easy to modify this assignment for any class. Sample annotations are provided in Figure 5.4.

Figure 5.3–What Is an Annotation?

An annotation is composed of three parts:

1. A summary of the contents of the book, if the book is fiction. Summaries answer the following questions. (This does not mean a summary is four sentences long, each sentence answering one of the questions but, rather, includes these four points.)

> Who is (are) the main character(s)?
> What is the problem?
> How does (do) the character(s) go about solving the problem?
> How does the story end?

2. A response by the reader to the book. A few sentences about how you felt about the reading and the book form the response portion of the annotation. If you are stuck for a response, you might address any of the following questions:

> Which character was most like you or someone you know and why?
> Which character did you despise and why?
> Has anything from the story ever happened to you?
> Would you recommend this book to someone to read and why/why not?
> Is this a book you would share with your mother and why/why not?
> How did you select this book?
> Would you read another book by this author and why/why not?
> What one scene had the greatest impact on you as a reader?
> Would this author make a good teacher and why/why not?
> If you were to give this book a one-word label, what would that be and why?

3. A bibliographic citation. Follow the bibliographic examples provided by the teacher and make sure that you record all that information at the beginning of the reading. If you forget to record the information, you can go to several online sources, particularly bookstores such as Amazon, to acquire any missing information.

Figure 5.4—Sample Annotations

Birdsall, Jeanne. *The Penderwicks: A Summer Tale of Four Sisters, Two Rabbits and a Very Interesting Boy.* Knopf, 2005. 272 pp. ISBN 0-375831436.

Meet the Penderwick sisters: Rosalind, age 12; Sky, 11; Jane 10; and Batty, 4. As usual, they are spending the summer with their dad vacationing. But this summer is full of surprises as they become friends with Jeffrey, the son of the woman who owns their cottage. Jeffrey's mother does not approve of his new friends, but that does not stop the sisters from having fun. I enjoyed how Rosalind and her sisters make ordinary things fun and how they got into trouble constantly. They are not the goody-goody kids I usually read about in books.

Levine, Gail Carson. *Fairy Dust and the Quest for the Egg.* Disney, 2005. 208 pp. ISBN 0-7868-3491-9.

The newest fairy to arrive in Neverland is Prilla. Prilla, though, does not really fit in with Tinkerbell and the other fairies because she does not know what her special talent is. Prilla finds out what she is supposed to do after a hurricane breaks Mother Dove's egg. Without her egg, Mother Dove begins to die. Her death will mean the end of Neverland. So Prilla must go on a quest to restore the egg and save Neverland. She will find her talent at the end of the quest. This book would go well with other books about Peter Pan and Tinkerbell like *Peter and the Starcatchers.* It was really quick to read and is also short.

Chalk Outline

A chalk outline is an un–book report that concentrates on character and can be done individually or in groups. Have students trace lifesize figures of bodies on butcher paper. These outlines can then be filled with words, images, or a combination, depending on your preferences. The bare outline has a head, two arms, two hands, two legs, and two feet. Additionally, I ask students to add a heart, some eyes, and a mouth. The area of the head is the place for students to insert words and images about the character's thoughts and ideas. These may be represented graphically, symbolically, or in other ways. The heart should reflect the feelings of the character. These feelings can be positive and negative. The eyes might represent the inner desires of the character or his or her innermost secrets. The mouth might have some of the important words spoken by the character, passages from the book, and so forth. For one of the hands, ask students to indicate actions this character took that were positive in terms of helping her or him overcome the problem of the novel. The other hand could indicate negative actions that hindered the resolution of the conflict. Arms should reflect things precious to the characters, things they might gather up should they come home to find a fire breaking out in their houses. Legs could symbolize the support the characters received from others in the story. Feet can be used to talk about literal (right) and figurative (left) journeys undertaken by the main character. Once these outlines are completed they can be hung on the walls or on the ceiling. Somewhere on the body students should write the title and author of their book.

Exposed or Undercover?

In my undergraduate classes, one of the things I try to emphasize to pre-service teachers is what I call the "quick and dirty" school of assignments. Veterans of the classroom know that anything assigned is also something that must be assessed, evaluated, or graded. It makes sense, then, to have some assignments that are quickly and easily dealt with. I would rather grade ten short annotations than one long summary or essay. So here is one more "quick and dirty" assessment that asks readers to think about reading at a higher level of comprehension. Here is the basic outline of this assignment.

Directions to Students

Before you open the book and begin reading, take several minutes to reflect on the cover of the book. Make a few descriptive notes (I provide sticky notes that students can place inside the front cover of the book) about what you see on the cover: title, author, illustration/graphic. Now, based on this observation, write one or two sentences that predict what you think will occur in this story.

After you finish reading the book, write a paragraph that compares your initial reflections and observations about the cover with your reflections and observations now that you have completed the reading. Does the title have a different meaning or significance? Is the illustration on the cover misleading or vague? How has the reading of the book affected your reaction to the cover?

Genre Exchange

Genre exchange is an idea I stole outright after hearing Kylene Beers talk about it in a presentation to teachers. Kylene discusses this idea (and many more) in *When Kids Can't Read: What Teachers Can Do* (2003). It has worked well with all ages and levels of kids, so I include it here. In addition, I offer two alternatives that I have developed in the last few years. Beers' genre exchange concept asks students to write a summary of a novel using a familiar format, such as a poem. Kylene, though, used the children's classic *Brown Bear, Brown Bear, What Do You See?* by Bill Martin. Using the rhythm and structure from this story, students talk about their novel. I like to do this for the first time in groups. I have the story in a big-book format, which I share with students before we begin our group work. I place students into groups of three or four and have all of them write a genre exchange over the same book. Interestingly, while there may be some similarities from group to group, each group generally produces a unique creation. Here is one example of a genre exchange using the novel *The Giver* by Lois Lowry.

> *Jonas, Jonas, what do you see?*
> *I see the Giver looking at me.*
> *Giver, Giver, what do you see?*
> *I see war hurting me.*
> *War, war, what do you see?*
> *I see a soldier dying for me.*
> *Soldier, soldier, what do you see?*
> *I see Jonas hurting for me.*
> *Jonas, Jonas what do you see.*
> *I see Gabriel needing me.*
> *Gabriel, Gabriel, what do you see?*
> *I see Jonas escaping with me.*
> *Jonas, Jonas, what do you see?*

An alternative to this basic genre exchange idea is to ask readers to create a wordless or textless picture book as their product. Contemporary kids are extremely visual. They have grown up with television and computers at the center of their lives. Much of their information comes to them visually. This explains the growing popularity of graphic novels and manga and anime. Tap into the interest in the visual and ask students to create a new format for the story. Share with the class several textless books that create a narrative. I would suggest David Wiesner's *Tuesday* in which a cadre of frogs arises via lily pads one fateful evening and descends upon an unsuspecting sleepy town. The frogs wreak some havoc before the enchantment wanes and they return once more to the pond, leaving the citizens puzzled. There is a lovely little surprise ending in store for readers as well. Once students see how pictures can narrate, they should be able to produce a textless or wordless book as one variation of the un–book report. Given that graphic novels and manga are popular, another variation of genre exchange would be to allow students to create such formats as well. Pop-up versions are also popular with tweens. This variation has one additional bonus: students can apply the mechanics of making pop-ups to reports they write for other classes or for history projects and science fairs. Math teachers will appreciate that making pop-ups requires careful measurement and some knowledge of geometry in some instances. Genre exchange has a multitude of applications.

Logs to Blogs

The reading log or book log is an idea that is not new in any sense of the word. Teachers have been using this alternative to traditional book reports for years. And, of course, that means there are literally dozens of variations on the standard concept of the log. I keep a running record of the books I read; otherwise, all the books would soon swim together into one conglomerate of a story. For a long time, I kept a traditional log—a spiral notebook—in which I recorded my thoughts and feelings as I read each successive book. There was no real structure to the log; I simply jotted down reactions and noted passages I enjoyed. I even commented on parts I disliked if I encountered them in a particular selection. As a teacher, I have used three basic approaches to the reading or book log.

One approach has a traditional structure with lots of parameters for the assignment. Basically, I asked students to pause at the end of each chapter and make some sort of comment, either a summary statement (if I was checking for comprehension) or some predictions for what might happen in a subsequent chapter (if it were important for me to develop that skill in the students). The log, kept in a spiral-bound notebook, was collected on a periodic basis. I made comments, gave a grade based upon the requirements of the assignment, and did very little to follow up on any entry that might have been made by a reader. With younger readers—and particularly at the beginning of the academic year—it is a good idea to offer the more traditional approach. Figure 5.5 offers one approach to reading logs.

Figure 5.5—Reading Log Directions

For each book read this grading period, you are to complete an entry in your reading log (spiral notebook). Please follow these directions in completing your reading log.

1. Attach on one blank page, your reading record (this is a simple recording of how many pages were read daily for this particular book). Be sure that you keep a running record during your reading of the book.
2. On the next page, create a bibliographic citation for the book using the example provided.
3. In the left margin, note the total number of pages in the book you read. (Note: I use this so students can easily tabulate how many pages they have read in a given period of time. I do not use this for assessment of any kind, but as one way to show students their progress at a glance.)
4. Pause at the end of each chapter (note: you can instead ask students to pause every certain number of pages, especially if the book has short chapters) and make a comment about the reading. You can summarize what has happened so far in the story, predict what might happen next, or make a response to the book. Remember to use your response guidelines (see below) if you do not know what to write.
5. Finally, after you have completed the reading of the entire book, write your personal evaluation of the book. Rate it against others you have read. How does it measure up? You can devise a scale of your own for the ratings.

RESPONSE GUIDELINES

Your response may take several forms: personal, interpretive, or critical. A personal response to the book comes from you as a reader. It asks you to explore your reactions to the book. How did the book make you feel? Did you experience some emotion (i.e., sorrow, happiness, frustration, anger, embarrassment)? Is there a character in the story with whom you can identify or empathize? Have you ever faced a situation that is similar? An interpretive response explores what you might do if you were involved in the story. If you were one of the characters in the book, what would you have done differently and why? At the critical level of response, you are focusing more on the text and the artistry of the author. Here you would comment on figurative language such as simile and metaphor. Is there a symbol being used by the author? What is it? How does it work?

Then, as the year progresses and students are more invested in the reading, it is possible to open up the assignment and make it less prescriptive and restrictive. For this form of book log, I might lift the requirement to stop every so many pages for a response. This alteration came about because of a comment I overheard one student make to another when they were talking about keeping a book log. This student was reading *Out of the Dust,* a novel in verse and Newbery Medal winner, by Karen Hesse. She was pausing at the end of every few pages to make an entry, something she found frustrating. "I am just getting into the story that's being told in the poem, and then I have to stop and write something. It kind of breaks up the story and I start to lose track of where I am." Even though it is essential to check that readers are comprehending the text as they read, it is a good idea to be flexible about how often a reader needs to pause and reflect or respond. Give students a few pieces of self-adhesive paper and ask them to quickly jot down reactions and responses as they read. They can either then put these into their spiral notebook, or you can ask them to complete another activity from their work. For example, once students have completed reading and have made notes on their sticky paper, they can organize and categorize their responses into a chart broken down into personal, interpretive, and critical comments.

Finally, we can offer students a new take on the old idea of logs: the blog. A blog is, in essence, a web log. Blogs are online logs, logs that are accessible by others. For years, I resolved to begin a blog. I finally did so, and am amazed at how much others enjoy reading the blogs and responding to me as a fellow reader (you can reach my blog at the following URL: www.livejournal.com/users/professornana). Again, this idea can be tailored to meet the needs of your individual classes. I blog once or twice a week. Sometimes I have little to report because I have not had a chance to read much. I might comment on a book I have finished reading, one that is sitting waiting for me to read, or one I have just begun to read.

I introduce the concept of blogging to students by doing one of my own over the course of a couple of months. Allow students access to your blogs and encourage them to comment on your entries. This blog can be mounted easily within your classroom computer, or you can opt for a blog at one of a number of sites that sponsor free blogging spaces. Basically, you are modeling what you expect of the students once their time to blog arrives. This approach works, in one regard, because it is new and involves the use of the computer. Bear in mind, though, that blogs will most likely have to be done during class time, since not all students have access to computers outside of school. Even if you do not involve students in blogging, keeping your own book blog will be rewarding and send a strong message to students that you are as much of a reader as you expect them to be.

Novel-Ties

Occasionally, doing something immediate and oral is a great way not only to change the focus of a book report, but to offer a chance for informal sharing in class—an activity that in and of itself is motivational. I read about a great activity on one of the listservs I frequent, YALSA-BK. On YALSA-BK, educators (mostly librarians) can talk about books for tweens and teens and related issues such as connecting kids to YA literature. One educator mentioned that she begins booktalks by pulling out a handful or two of her husband's old neckties and asking kids to select one of the ties and talk about why that tie reminds her or him of a book he or she has read recently. Now that my husband is happily retired, he has quite a few retired neckties that run the gamut from staid and traditional to wildly colorful to downright ugly. I take ten or twelve of them into the classroom at the beginning of class and ask students whether they see a tie that reminds them of a book they have read recently. In the past, students have selected a yellow tie with red stripes and talked about one of the Harry Potter books because the colors are those of one of the Hogwarts houses. A turquoise tie with kittens prancing on it reminded a student of a book where the main character was dealing with so many problems that it was akin to "juggling kittens." Another student selected a tie she could envision on Count Olaf from the Lemony Snicket books.

Once students have had the time to connect with one of the ties, the informal sharing about books can continue by asking kids to volunteer to talk about what they are reading that they really like or dislike. Of course, it is essential that the teacher also be an active participant in this process. I recall telling a group of students once that even though I really disliked the book I was reading, I felt compelled to read it because it had been awarded a Newbery Medal. Several members of the class asked if they could read the book after I was through to see whether they agreed with my opinion. While I seldom waste time talking about books I do not like, I can see the merit in showing students that not all books are good for all readers, and that just because a book has received an award does not mean it is a "good" book for me or for all readers either.

Sticky-Note Poetry

Sticky-note poetry began when I neglected to remove some sticky tabs from a book of poetry I had been reading before I placed the book in circulation for the rest of the class to read. The book was *I Feel a Little Jumpy Around You: A Book of Her Poems and His Poems Collected in Pairs* edited by Paul Janeczko and Naomi Shihab Nye. Whenever I read books of stories or poems, I keep a pad of sticky tabs nearby to mark passages and poems that speak to me in some way. Then I make a copy of the poems, remove the sticky tabs, and place the book on the shelf for others to peruse. This time I forgot to remove the tabs and a student checked out the book. When she returned it to me, I noticed a lot more tabs. She told me and the class that she had decided to mark her favorite poems in the same way but elected to use a different-color tab so we could see where we as readers agreed and disagreed. Suddenly, there was a demand for sticky tabs as other students borrowed the book and used their own colors to mark favorites. By the time the book had circulated a few times, there was barely a page left unmarked. We were also able to quickly assess the class favorites because they sported a variety of colored flags. So what began as an error morphed into one of my favorite things to do with poetry collections.

This idea can readily be adapted to other situations. Since kids love sticky flags, tabs, and notes (and so do I), I keep a supply on hand. From time to time, I ask them to mark favorite passages with stickies and then place the book back on the shelf for others to find. Teachers could ask readers to mark a passage that they think best serves to show character, a scene that would prompt an immediate reaction from another reader, or a chapter they think best conveys the conflict faced by the main characters. Another variation of this strategy would be to have each student jot notes on stickies as they read. At the end of the reading, they can transfer these notes to another template or worksheet, categorizing the notes in categories such as: Questions I Had as I Read, Emotional Reactions, Words I Did Not Know, and so on. This compilation of sticky notes forms a sort of reading log. If a local business wants to adopt the school or classroom or when a parent asks what she or he might contribute to my classroom, I always request sticky materials because they are inexpensive and versatile.

PowerPoint® Booktalks

Corrie spends hours of time in her room creating elaborate PowerPoint® slides, mostly for her own entertainment. She always opts for PowerPoint® projects in her classes. She thinks these projects are fun simply because she can use this software. Corrie is not alone in her fascination with PowerPoint®; most students enjoy it. So why not use this attraction as another alternative to the traditional book report? Students create a PowerPoint® presentation intended to motivate someone else to read the book. My friend and master librarian, Lois Buckman, uses kid-generated PowerPoint® booktalks in the library. As students file in for their regular visits to the library, Lois plays the various PowerPoint® slides on a computer. One student had a screen dissolve for *In the Forests of the Night* by Amelia Atwater-Rhodes that dripped blood onto the screen, apropos for this vampire novel. Some used sound effects and graphics to heighten the attraction factor of the presentations. Imagine how many of these might be accumulated over the course of a school year and then used with each successive class in the years to come. Again, like most of the ideas here, this assignment could be structured in many different ways. Teachers could ask students to include slides that describe the main characters or slides that provide information about setting, conflict, and other aspects of plot. Students could include appropriate music that would set the mood for the story or use clip art to tell a scene of the story without words. There is no end to the many ways this idea might be adapted.

Shelf Markers and Shelf Talkers

Keeping kids connected to books is one of the critical aspects of creating lifetime readers. While booktalks to the class, book shares with individual students, visits to the library, and other techniques help it is not always possible to be in the one spot where a student might need some guidance. The shelf marker was born out of a sense of desperation. What, I asked, could I do to help all students find books they would enjoy reading? I know there is value in having class time simply for informal sharing of what we are currently reading. I begin each of my university classes with this sharing time. Frequently, as one student talks about a book, another is reaching over to grab it; there is something inherently powerful in the recommendation of a peer. But I could not do this as often as I wanted. Then, one day I was walking through one of my favorite bookstores in Houston, where the employees set aside a shelf on which they place their current favorites along with a short note about why they like the book. Hey, I thought, I could do that. So, I designated the top shelf of the classroom bookcase for this concept. Different groups of students take turns creating their own shelf markers for a week or two throughout the school year. Their task is to collect their favorite books, write a few sentences about why they are favorites, and create a display to catch their classmates' attention. The groups can be established by using literature circles or another method.

An alternative to the concept of the shelf marker popped into my head when I received a personalized computer birthday card, where the sender recorded a personal message on a tiny microchip in the card. I took that chip, let students record a brief book blurb on it, then placed that in the shelf-marker display, too. This proved to be popular, and I haunted the discount stores searching for cards that had the chip. Press the button, and instant booktalk!

It is simple to do: the chip is glued into the card. Remove the microchip. Most chips have a tab or smallish button to depress so that a message can be recorded. Record the brief booktalk blurb and then adhere the chip to a card or another part of the shelf marker. There are other venues for finding these chips. Most of the stores that permit someone to personalize a stuffed animal have chips that can also carry recorded messages. They are not terribly expensive and can be purchased separately. Finally, an audioclip can be downloaded to a CD or MP3 player and used as part of the shelf talking display.

SWBST: Somebody Wanted But So Then

SWBST works well in several different situations. At the beginning of the school year, we read a novel together to establish our processes and routines for reading and talking about books, then I assign a chapter to be read at home. The next morning is a time of apprehension: did everyone read the chapter? SWBST is a quick way to assess this reading. Ask students to create five columns on a sheet of paper. At the top of each column they write the following words: Somebody, Wanted, But, So, and Then. In the Somebody column, students write the name of the main character or characters. What that character wants goes in the next column. Note that the "want" could be concrete things such as a car or tickets to a concert or the "want" could be more abstract such as respect or fortune. The But column introduces the problem or conflict of the story and So asks students what the character does or will do to overcome the conflict. Finally, Then requires that students make a prediction about what might happen next. This activity takes a matter of moments to complete and is an easy way to assess whether or not students have completed the reading. From the five columns, a logical next step could be to ask students to write a brief statement summarizing this first chapter and using the words they noted in the columns.

Other variations could include asking students to complete the columns each time they complete a chapter. These columns come in handy when writing annotations, summaries, and traditional book reports as well. Students can also concentrate on only one column in order to report in some form about characters, conflict, motivations, and so forth.

Ugly Book Contest

Kandi Kauk, from Sinton, Texas, teams up with her school librarian each year for the ugly book contest. Alice, the librarian scours the shelves for books whose covers lack tween appeal but whose contents are both appropriate for tweens and provide them with satisfying reading experiences. Kandi and the librarian booktalk the books and allow students to select one that they will "adopt." Adoption is a two-step process; first the student reads the chosen book and then designs a new cover that will make the book more glamorous. The cover is first planned and sketched. Then the new cover is made, laminated, and put on the book. Here is one possible planning sheet that might be provided to students involved in the Ugly Book Contest.

Figure 5.6—Planning a Glam Cover for Your Book

All book covers have five parts that need to be completed before the new cover can be applied to the book. Use this sheet to plan your final design. Be certain to complete all sections and get approval from your teacher before you proceed to the final cover design.

SECTION ONE: SPINE

The information needed for this part of the cover is simple: the author's last name, the title, and the publisher. This information will be arranged from the top of the spine to the bottom. Try different typefaces to find one that would be most attractive. Remember, sometimes the first thing a reader sees is the spine of the book. Plan now what color the cover will be as well.

Figure 5.6–Planning a Glam Cover for Your Book (cont.)

SECTION TWO: FRONT FLAP

The inside front cover of the book is intended to lure readers into the book. It is partly summary, but does not give away too much of the story (otherwise, why would we want to read it?). Generally, it teases prospective readers with questions. Read several examples of front-flap summaries that your teacher provides and use those as a model for your book's flap. Your space and word count is limited here, so try to be as brief and interesting as possible. It might be a good idea to try your copy out on a classmate for her or his reaction.

SECTION THREE: BACK FLAP

The inside back cover of the book is generally where information about the author can be found. It is customary to include a snapshot of the author here. There are several places to look for information about your author. You can certainly get information from the book you have adopted. You can also check online at several places bookmarked by the librarian for updated information and photographs. The library has other reference materials that can assist you in your search for information. Try to make the author information as exciting as you can for your readers.

SECTION FOUR: BACK COVER

For this assignment, the back cover of the book needs to have reviews of the author's other books (if there are other books by this author) or reviews of this book. The reviews can come from established sources such as reviewing journals (and some of this material can be found at amazon.com) or you can interview other readers about this book and include their quotes on the back cover.

SECTION FIVE: FRONT COVER

As you know, this can make or break a book. So careful planning is essential before you move on to this last step in designing. The cover needs to have the title and author's full name as well as some sort of design, drawing, graphic, illustration, or painting. Decisions about typeface and type size are important here, too. You can create original art, use clip art from several sources, or find photos and pictures from magazines and other sources.

Gradually, over the years, Kandi and her librarian have done away with many of the ugly books and brought a new generation of readers to their pages. The possibilities are, literally, endless. What motivates one student or class may differ for another student or class. It is wise to have on hand several alternative books from which students can pick and choose over the course of the year and from year to year.

afterword

Naked reading continues at our house nightly. Natalie disappears into the bathroom for her nightly quiet reading time, and Corrie, her grandfather, and I dive into books as often as time allows. During the vigil around Hurricane Rita, we whiled away muggy hours without electricity, reading by candlelight and flashlight. Naked reading extends well beyond our house. A colleague of mine meted out listening to an audiobook I loaned her as she evacuated the Houston area in anticipation of the same hurricane, during the hundred-mile trip that took twelve hours due to horrendous traffic jams. School closures before and after the hurricane gave all of us precious time for naked reading of anything that appealed to us. We were able to enjoy the essential elements of naked reading: plenty of books and time to read them.

Of course, motivating kids to read is not just a matter of providing them with books and time. We must also be aware of which strategies and activities will work with our kids—what we can do to make the act of reading more palatable and more enjoyable. We need to always be on the lookout for the kinds of books our students embrace, and understand that tastes and interests can change from class to class and year to year and even moment to moment. Finding the books that speak to our students means paying attention to details like popular topics for nonfiction, issues of importance to tweens, and variables such as gender, age, and other developmental aspects that can affect choice in reading material.

All educators—teachers, librarians, and any other people involved in creating readers—need to realize that they have tremendous power to alter the life of any child. When we find books that meet the needs and interests of our students, we are placing them squarely on the road to a lifetime of reading. We never know how one right book at the right time in the right hands might impact a tween. One final thing to remember is this: if we ourselves are models of literacy, we can also impact students simply by our own behavior.

Sometime last year, a librarian in South Carolina came up to me at the end of a workshop and told me she was going to email me a poem I would appreciate. How I wish I could remember the wonderful person who sent me the following poem. It speaks volumes to me and to all whose hope it is to connect kids to books and reading. I place it here at the end of this book in the hope that it will speak to all of you about the important work we do.

To the Woman (We Think You're a Teacher) with the Books on the 2 Train

By some anonymous students

On the platform for the 2 train
you stand with a book in your hand
the pages open
Which is how you enter the train
Reading

Sometimes you smile, or frown
Once you even cried
on the train
when you were reading *Night*
and a man sitting across the aisle
said he cried too, when he read that book
and we thought,
we want to read that book
so we did

And then you were reading all those
basketball books

by Walter Dean Myers
so we read those too
speeding along on the 2 train
one time you saw us reading *Slam*
and you said
I love that book
and do you think Slam is going to make it in high
school?
We do, we think he's going to make it

Then you were reading some really hard stuff
*Epistemology of the Closet, Postmodern Narrative
Theory*
and we tried those, but we think you have to have read
the books those authors have read, if you want to read
their books

Our favorite is when you are reading poetry
Picnic, Lightning
and you lean back against the seat
and smile
and keep reading the same page
again and again
we do that now and it's really nice

Last week you were reading *Life of Pi*
and we rushed out to buy it
So we could be in the lifeboat
adrift in the blue, blue sea
with the boy, the Bengal Tiger, and you

If we don't see you next year
on the train
Maybe sometime we'll bump into each other on the
platform
You'll know us because
we'll have books in our hands.

May we all be that woman or man on the train who reaches out to an unseen audience and perhaps convinces them that there is a world to discover in books.

appendix

More Than One Hundred
Great Books for Tweens

Here are some outstanding books for tween readers, many published within the past five years. I have indicated at the end of the brief annotation whether the books are more suitable for all readers (ALL), for intermediate readers, grades 4–5 (INT), or for middle school readers, grades 6–8 (MS). A few are designated for more mature readers (MMR) in eighth and ninth grades. In some cases, more than one audience designation is provided. It is difficult to pigeonhole a book as a fourth-grade book or an eighth-grade book. Overall, books range in appeal according to the age of the reader. These designations indicate the *potential* audience. It is up to each teacher to determine not only the needs and interests of her or his students, but also to determine the development of those children. I take into account the typical development of each age range when I make my recommendations. Please note also that some books suggested both for middle school (MS) and for more mature readers (MMR) should be directed toward mature middle school readers. These are only suggested guidelines. Teachers need to preview *all* books before placing them on their shelves to circulate in the classroom. Of course, selecting those books that meet the stated preferences, needs, and interests of your students is best. I routinely asked my classes what books and materials I should be adding to the classroom library.

In addition to these books, consult the lists published annually by the American Library Association. Best Books for Young Adults (BBYA) is a listing of books published each year that a committee of librarians deem as the best we have to offer young adults. The Quick Picks (QP) list is designated for reluctant readers and is also an annual list. The Notable Books for Children list cites quality books for readers from the very young to the young adult. These lists, in addition to the books that win the Newbery, Coretta Scott King and Printz Awards, are one way of identifying potential new books for the classroom library and for classroom study and discussion. You can find these lists by accessing ALA's home page (www.ala.org) and following the links.

Other professional organizations also provide annual lists of noteworthy books. The Children's Book Council (www.cbcbooks.org) provides links to lists such as Notable Trade Books in Science and Notable Trade Books in Social Studies. These content-area books could be one way of creating interdisciplinary units of study with a book at the center of the theme or unit. The National Council of Teachers of English annually produces Notable Trade Books in the Language Arts and makes awards in the areas of poetry and nonfiction. You can access these lists at their Web site (www.ncte.org). Finally, the International Reading Association (www.reading.org) conducts several book projects annually, most notably Children's Choices, YA Choices, and Teachers' Choices.

One final note: many kids in lower grades are already reading YA titles. When YA literature burst onto the scene in the late sixties and early seventies, its readership was older teens. Now, many of the newest titles in YA literature are labeled ages ten and up. While this is partly marketing, there is still some truth to the label. Kids are reading YA literature in fourth and fifth grades. By sixth and seventh, many of them have moved onto authors and titles once considered for older readers. *The Outsiders* by S. E. Hinton has become part of the middle school canon. Natalie is reading Chris Crutcher at age twelve. She seems to find this interesting and appropriate material. We talk about the books she reads, and I do think she understands the more complex themes of these books once designated for high school–aged readers. So, while this list might seem to be weighted toward older readers, it is truly more of a reflection of what kids are reading out there in the real world.

Almond, David. *The Fire-Eaters*. Delacorte Press, 2004. Bobby Burns comes face-to-face with several demons as he enters high school, a time when the Cuban missile crisis is causing some panic in America and abroad. Also by this author: *Skellig* and *Kit's Wilderness*. (MS)

Appelt, Kathi. *Kissing Tennessee: And Other Stories from the Stardust Dance*. Harcourt, 2004. This realistic portrayal of the hopes and dreams of an array of teens at a school dance is certain to touch resonant chords, particularly with girls. This story collection deals with themes of love, betrayal, loss, family, and much more. (MS)

Appelt, Kathi. *My Father's Summers: A Daughter's Memoir.* Holt, 2004. In lyrical prose, Kathi tells of how her life was altered when her parents divorced and her dad remarried. (MS)

Atwater-Rhodes, Amelia. *Demon in My View.* Delacorte Press, 2000. This sequel to *In the Forests of the Night* is another vampire novel written by a teen author. Consider this as an alternative to requests for a Buffy the Vampire Slayer novel. *Hawksong* is one of the books in a new series about shape shifters that will also appeal to fans of the vampire novels. (MS)

Avi. *Poppy.* HarperTrophy, 2005. Poppy, a timid dormouse, volunteers to scout a new home for the growing mouse population of Dimwood Forest. She hopes to expose the leader of the forest, Ocax, for the bully he truly is. Also in this series: *Poppy And Rye, Ragweed,* and *Ereth's Birthday.* (INT)

Avi. *Something Upstairs.* HarperTrophy, 1997. Twelve-year-old Kenny moves into an ancient house to discover that it is haunted by the ghost of a murdered teenage slave named Caleb. Kenny must travel back in time to help solve Caleb's murder. (MS)

Balliett, Blue. *Chasing Vermeer.* Scholastic Press, 2004. Think of this as *The Da Vinci Code* for younger readers and you have some idea of the complexity of the mystery at the core of this novel. (INT/MS)

Barker, Clive. *Abarat.* HarperCollins, Joanna Cotler Books, 2002. Fantasy about a girl's journey to Abarat. This is planned as a series of adventures for Candy Quackenbush. Oil paintings by the author, included in the text, are the basis for the story. (MS)

Bauer, Cat. *Harley, Like a Person.* Winslow Press, 2000. Harley is certain she must be adopted. How could she be the product of her parents? A startling discovery leads her to New York and some answers about her past. (MS)

Bauer, Joan. *Backwater.* G. P. Putnam's, 1999. In the Breedlove family, there is only one career: law. Ivy Breedlove, though, is more interested in history; specifically, the history of her family. When she discovers an errant relative, she is determined to find her. (MS/MMR)

Bauer, Joan. *Hope Was Here.* G. P. Putnam's Sons, 2000. Hope is a waitress who is less than thrilled with the move to the "Land of Lactose." Political intrigue and blossoming romance may change her mind. Newbery Honor winner. (MS/MMR)

Bauer, Joan. *Stand Tall.* G. P. Putnam's Sons, 2002. Living between mom's apartment and dad's house proves a bit more than Tree can bear. (MS)

Benton, Jim. *Dear Dumb Diary, Let's Pretend This Never Happened.* Scholastic, 2004. Jamie is a middle school student forced to keep a diary with hilarious and predictable results. Luckily, this is also part of a series for those readers who demand another book "just like this one." (INT)

Bloor, Edward. *Story Time.* Harcourt, 2004. George and Kate are sent to the new Whittaker Magnet School, a school for genius children. Kate feels out of place until she meets a secretive librarian. (INT/MS)

Blume, Judy. *Are You There, God? It's Me, Margaret.* Laurel Leaf, 1991. Margaret Simon worries about growing up and fitting in, into her bra, that is, in this classic coming-of-age story written more than thirty years ago. Also by Blume: *Then Again Maybe I Won't, Blubber, Deenie, Tales of a Fourth Grade Nothing,* and *Iggie's House.* (INT/MS).

Bode, Janet. *The Colors of Freedom: Immigrant Stories.* Franklin Watts, 2000. Nonfiction book about the struggles and triumphs of students who have emigrated from other countries will provide real insights for readers. Check out other books by Janet Bode if you are looking for excellent nonfiction to share with your readers. (MS)

Brashares, Ann. *Sisterhood of the Traveling Pants.* Delacorte, 2001. One pair of pants and four friends make for a memorable summer in this quirky coming-of-age story. There are sequels! (MS/MMR)

Brooks, Bruce. *Throwing Smoke.* HarperTrophy, 2002. This is a lighthearted fantasy about a manager who invents some talent for his little league team, literally. Young male readers will like the fact that this is a *short* book, too. (INT/MS)

Byars, Betsy. *The Summer of the Swans.* Viking, 1970. Sara loves her brother Charlie but caring for him sometimes can be too much responsibility. When Charlie disappears, Sara fears the worst has happened and she is to blame. (MS)

Byars, Betsy. *The Eighteenth Emergency.* Puffin, 1981. Twelve-year-old Mouse has an enormous set of obstacles facing him, the most pressing of which is that the school bully has sworn to kill him. None of the plans Mouse has for handling other emergencies can help him with this one. (INT)

Cabot, Meg. *All American Girl.* HarperTrophy, 2003. When she saves the life of the president of the United States, Samantha Madison has no idea of how much her life will change. (MS/MMR)

Cart, Michael (ed.). *911: The Book of Help.* Cricket Books, 2002. Authors share their responses to the tragic events of September 11. (MS/MMR)

Cheng, Andrea. *Honeysuckle House.* Front Street, 2004. Best friends Sarah and Victoria are separated suddenly. To compound Sarah's troubles, she is forced to befriend a new student from China even though she speaks not a word of Chinese. (INT)

Choldenko. Gennifer. *Al Capone Does My Shirts.* Putnam, 2004. Set in 1935 on Alcatraz Island, this is the story of a young boy dealing with his autistic sister and his new apartment on the prison grounds. Newbery Honor winner. (INT/MS)

Cleary, Beverly. *Dear Mr. Henshaw.* Morrow Junior Books, 1983. This Newbery Medal book consists of a series of letters that Leigh writes to his teacher. In the process, he learns to cope with his parents' divorce and with going to a new school. The sequel is *Strider.* (INT/MS)

Clements, Andrew. *Things Not Seen.* Philomel Books, 2002. Bobby wakes up invisible one morning. Complications arise when his parents are injured in a car accident. How can his absence be explained? (MMR)

Clements, Andrew. *Lunch Money.* Simon & Schuster, 2005. Greg Kenton has always been good with money. Once he realizes that most of his classmates always have some spare change, he hits on a way to make some serious dough. Unfortunately, there will be some obstacles along the way to fame and fortune. Also by the author, *The Landry News, The Report Card, The Jacket,* and *The School Story.* (INT)

Colfer, Eoin. *The Wish List.* Hyperion, 2003. Meg Finn, to atone for her life of crime, must help an elderly man accomplish everything on his wish list. (INT/MS)

Colfer, Eoin. *The Supernaturalist.* Hyperion, 2004. This futuristic novel about a group of children fighting an invisible enemy only they can see is a great introduction to science fiction for students. (MS/MMR)

Corder, Zizou. *Lion Boy: The Chase.* Dial Books, 2004. This sequel to *Lion Boy* tells how Charlie Ashanti manages to smuggle a pride of lions from a train to their homeland. Loads of danger and adventure will make readers ask to read the first book in this trilogy. (INT/MS)

Cormier, Robert. *Frenchtown Summer.* Dell Laurel-Leaf, 2001. A young boy's summer in his native town is presented in blank verse by one of our most talented authors. (MS)

Cormier, Robert. *The Rag and Bone Shop.* Delacorte Press, 2001. This is his final novel and is vintage Cormier. Jason is a young man facing a clever police interrogator who will not stop until he secures a confession about a brutal murder. How far are the police willing to go for a conviction? (MS/MMR)

Couloumbis, Audrey. *Getting Near to Baby.* Putnam, 1999. When Mama loses her baby, two young girls are sent off to live with relatives. The closest they can come to getting close to baby is to climb out on the roof and gaze at the stars above them. Newbery Honor winner. (MS)

Couloumbis, Audrey. *Say Yes.* Putnam, 2002. A young girl, abandoned by her one living relative, must take chances in order to stay free from the child welfare system. (MS/MMR)

Coville, Bruce. *Odder Than Ever.* Harcourt, 2000. Throw out the literature books. Use one or more of these "odd" stories by Coville and you will have them hooked. "The Stinky Princess" is sure to be a hit. (INT/MS)

Coville, Bruce. *My Teacher Is an Alien.* Aladdin, 2005. Susan, age twelve, is certain that her favorite teacher has been replaced by an alien disguised as a human. Also in this series: *My Teacher Glows in the Dark, My Teacher Flunked the Planet,* and *Aliens Ate My Homework.* (INT/MS)

Creech, Sharon. *Love That Dog.* HarperTrophy, 2003. This slim novel in verse tells the story of Jack and his beloved dog, Sky, in a series of poems. (INT/MS)

Creech, Sharon. *Heartbeat.* HarperCollins, 2004. A novel in verse tells of Annie's love of running and her excitement about the prospective birth of her baby brother. (INT/MS)

Creech, Sharon. *Granny Torrelli Makes Soup.* HarperTrophy, 2005. Tight lyrical prose tells of the warm relationship between Rosie, Bailey, and Granny Torrelli. (INT/MS)

Crowe, Chris. *Mississippi Trial, 1955.* Putnam, 2002. The kidnapping and drowning of a young African American in a small Mississippi town is the real-life basis for this historical novel. IRA Book Award. Direct readers to the nonfiction story of Emmett Till, also by Chris Crowe. (MS)

Crowe, Chris. *Getting Away with Murder: The True Story of the Emmett Till Case.* Putnam Books, 2003. In 1954, fourteen-year-old Emmett Till was visiting relatives in Mississippi where he was murdered for flirting with a white woman. This book chronicles the crime and the trial of the white men who killed him. (MS/MMR)

Cruise, Robin. *Fiona's Private Pages.* Harcourt, 2002. This sequel follows Fiona after her parents' divorce. The format of the book is the diary kept by Fiona as she deals with the impending divorce. (INT/MS)

Curtis, Christopher Paul. *The Watsons Go to Birmingham, 1963.* Delacorte Press, 1995. Although Kenny's account of the Watson family trip from Flint Michigan to Alabama is humorous, the civil unrest of the 1960s is evident. Also by the author: *Bud, Not Buddy.* (INT)

Curtis, Christopher Paul. *Bucking the Sarge*. Wendy Lamb Books, 2004. Luther Farrell has a former drill sergeant for a mother and a whole heap of trouble when he dares to challenge her. (MS)

Cushman, Karen. *Rodzina*. Clarion Books, 2003. This historical novel examines the life of a young girl placed on the Orphan Train and headed west to find a new family. Rodzina fears her future will be one of servitude. (INT/MS)

Danziger, Paula, and Ann M. Martin. *Snail Mail No More*. Scholastic Press, 2000. Another sequel, this one tells the story of two best friends through a series of e-mails. Direct readers to the first book by this dynamic duo: *P.S. Longer Letter Later: A Novel in Letters*. (INT/MS)

Danziger, Paula. *United Tates Of America: A Novel with Scrapbook Art*. Scholastic, 2002. This novel with scrapbook art is quintessential Danziger: warm and humorous with shades of poignancy. (INT)

Davis, Jill (ed.). *Open Your Eyes: Extraordinary Experiences In Faraway Places*. Viking, 2003. This short-story collection about travel will help readers understand that travel can open up new worlds and experiences for them. (MS/MMR)

DiCamillo, Kate. *Because of Winn-Dixie*. Candlewick Press, 2000. Winn-Dixie is a dog that manages to bring happiness into the lives of many in this small community. No, the dog does not die! Note: there is a movie tie-in for this title. (INT/MS)

DiCamillo, Kate. *The Miraculous Journey of Edward Tulane*. Candlewick Press, 2006. Edward Tulane, a china rabbit, comes to understand why love is so important in the lives of us all in this mesmerizing fantasy. (INT)

DiCamillo, Kate. *The Tale of Despereaux: Being the Story of a Mouse, a Princess, Some Soup, and a Spool of Thread*. Candlewick Press, 2003. A mouse falls in love with a princess and ventures into the dungeon to rescue her when she is kidnapped by a rat. This is an excellent choice as a read-aloud book with its short chapters and cliffhanger endings. Also look for the chapter that discusses how cause and effect have played a crucial role in the story. (INT/MS)

Dowell, Frances O'Roark. *Dovey Coe*. Atheneum, 2000. Dovey is twelve and stands accused of murder. Her first-person narrative is great for a lesson on *voice*. (MS)

DuPrau, Jeanne. *The People of Sparks*. Random House, 2004. Sequel to *City of Ember* shows how two groups of people must learn to get along and share.

For students who are not quite ready to tackle the futuristic world of Lois Lowry's *The Giver,* this book might prove to be a gateway. (MS)

Ferris, Jean. *Of Sound Mind.* Farrar, Straus and Giroux, 2001. Theo is the only hearing person in his family. As a result, he has been the chief means of communication for his deaf parents and brother. When he meets Ivy, he discovers a friend in a similar situation. (MS/MMR)

Fine, Anne. *Up on Cloud Nine.* Delacorte Press, 2002. When his best friend lands in the hospital, Ian has time to consider their friendship. (MS)

Finklestein, Norman H. *The Way Things Never Were: The Truth About the Good Old Days.* Atheneum, 1999. If you are old enough to use this phrase, you need this book. If you are tired of hearing this phrase, you need this book. Either way, this book is a winner! (MS/MMR)

Flake, Sharon G. *Who Am I Without Him? Short Stories About Girls and the Boys in Their Lives.* Jump at the Sun/Hyperion, 2004. Flake's collection touches on all aspects of boy-girl relationships. Also by the author; *The Skin I'm In* and *Bang!* a Coretta Scott King Honor winner. (MS/MMR)

Fleischman, John. *Phineas Gage: A Gruesome but True Story About Brain Science.* Houghton Mifflin, 2002. Phineas Gage survives when a piece of iron shoots through his cheek and brain. He becomes a medical marvel. This piece of nonfiction examines what we have learned about the brain and its lobes and hemispheres as a result of Gage's accident. (INT/MS)

Fox, Helen. *Eager.* Wendy Lamb Books, 2004. EGR3 is the new family robot. At first, Gavin and Fleur are not certain they like this new robot. However, EGR3's role in the family will become of prime importance later. This easily accessible science fiction story introduces readers to Socrates and contains more than a bit of humor. (MS)

Frost, Helen. *Keesha's House.* Farrar, Straus and Giroux, 2003. In sestina and sonnets, the author tells of several troubled teens who all find respite and hope in Keesha's house. (MS/MMR)

Funke, Cornelia. *The Thief Lord.* Scholastic, 2002. Set in Venice, this story is reminiscent of the writings of Charles Dickens. Two orphaned boys join up with an older, masked man who gives them a place to live in exchange for their assistance in stealing things. (MS)

Funke, Cornelia. *Inkheart.* Scholastic, 2003. What happens when someone can read characters to life from books? This story combines elements of fantasy and adventure. A sequel, *Inkspell,* is new. (INT/MS)

Funke, Cornelia. *Dragon Rider.* Scholastic, 2004. A young dragon, Firedrake, is joined on a dangerous journey by an orphaned boy named Ben, a brownie named Sorrel, and a creature known as a homunculus, who is serving as a spy for the evil Nettlebrand. (INT)

Gaiman, Neil. *Coraline.* HarperCollins, 2002. This spooky mystery about an alternate universe with troubling inhabitants is certain to be a favorite read-aloud. Coraline's parents become trapped in their new flat, and she must rescue them. (MS)

Gaiman, Neil. *The Day I Swapped My Dad for Two Goldfish.* HarperCollins, 2004. Gaiman's picture books like this one and *The Wolves in the Wall* are perfect for older readers. (INT/MS)

Gallo, Donald R. (ed.). *On the Fringe.* Speak, 2003. This collection of stories examines what it is like to be a teen pushed to the fringe by bullies. Outstanding stories by Joan Bauer, Jack Gantos, Chris Crutcher, and others. (MS/MMR)

Gallo, Donald R. (ed.). *First Crossing: Stories About Teen Immigrants.* Candlewick Press, 2004. Award-winning YA authors write stories about teens facing more than the usual problems. Other Gallo collections such as *Short Circuits, Within Reach,* and *Connections* are good selections as well. (MS/MMR)

Gantos. Jack. *Joey Pigza Loses Control.* Farrar, Straus and Giroux, 2000. Joey goes off for the summer with his dad and tries to be the best son he can. This sequel to *Joey Pigza Swallowed the Key* shines all on its own. Newbery Honor winner. (INT/MS)

Gantos, Jack. *What Would Joey Do?* Farrar, Straus and Giroux, 2002. Third and final installment in the Joey Pigza story has Joey trying to deal with feuding parents, an obnoxious blind girl, home schooling and a Chihuahua kidnapper. (INT/MS)

Gantos, Jack. *Jack Adrift: Fourth Grade Without a Clue.* Farrar Straus and Giroux, 2003. The final installment in the Jack book series finds Jack's family moved to a trailer while his dad works for the Navy. Part of the Jack Henry series, there are books with Jack in fourth through eighth grade. (INT/MS)

Ghigna, Charles. *Fury of Motion: Poems for Boys.* Sagebrush, 2003. Poems range in subject from baseball to first love to friendship. (INT/MS)

Giff, Patricia Reilly. *Pictures of Hollis Woods.* Random House, 2002. Hollis has been bounced from one foster home to another until she comes to know and love the Regans. (INT/MS)

Gilmore, Rachna. *A Group of One.* Holt, 2001. Tara is upset when the history teacher does not think she is a Canadian simply because some of her relatives emigrated from India. However, Tara gains new pride in her Indian heritage when she learns of her grandmother's involvement in the Quit India Movement. (MS)

Glenn, Mel. *Split Image: A Story in Poems.* HarperCollins, 2000. Laura Li is torn between two cultures. Her story is told from many different people's points of view. Glenn offers other novels in verse such as *Who Killed Mr. Chippendale?, The Taking of Room 114, Jump Ball,* and *Foreign Exchange.* (MS/MMR)

Glover, Savion, with Bruce Weber. *Savion: My Life in Tap.* Morrow, 2000. This autobiography focuses more on dance than strictly on Glover. Great photos! (ALL)

Grandits, John. *Technically, It's Not My Fault: Concrete Poems.* Clarion, 2004. Hilarious poems about falling blocks and farts are the subject of this collection sure to win tons of readers over to the genre. Tie this one to *A Poke in the I* by Paul Janeczko, illustrated by Chris Raschka. (INT/MS)

Gutman, Dan. *Funny Boy Versus the Bubble-Brained Barbers from the Big Bang.* Hyperion, 2000. Doesn't the title say it all? A short and funny chapter book, part of a series from Hyperion focusing on younger male readers in particular. Also by the author: *Abner and Me, Mickey and Me,* My Weird School series. (INT/MS)

Hale, Marian. *The Truth About Sparrows.* Holt, 2004. Historical fiction set during the Depression in Texas' Gulf Coast tells of Sadie's life when she and her family are forced to leave their home in Missouri and move to Texas. In Texas, Sadie faces many obstacles, especially at her new school. (INT/MS)

Hannigan, Katherine. *Ida B. . . and Her Plans to Maximize Fun, Avoid Disaster, and (Possibly) Save the World.* Greenwillow Books, 2004. For the first time, Ida B must leave home and attend the school in her neighborhood. Can she manage to deal with this new environment, her mother's battle with cancer, and other new challenges? (INT)

Hartman, Holly. *Girlwonder: Every Girl's Guide to the Fantastic Feats, Cool Qualities, and Remarkable Abilities of Women and Girls.* Houghton Mifflin, 2003. What more could I add? (MS/MMR)

Haseley, Dennis. *Trick of the Eye.* Dial Books, 2004. Richard has noticed that if he stares intently at a painting, he can hear the people on canvas converse. They have a mystery only he can solve. (MS)

Hawes, Louise. *Waiting for Christopher.* Candlewick Press, 2002. When she sees a little boy being abused, she decides she must rescue him by any means. (MS)

Henkes, Kevin. *The Birthday Room.* Greenwillow Books, 1999. When his parents present him with his very own room in which to create works of art, Ben is less than thrilled. Somehow the room means more. A surprise letter from an uncle gone from his life for a decade may change the function of the room. Also by the author: *Sun and Spoon, Protecting Marie,* and *Words of Stone.* (INT/MS)

Henkes, Kevin. *Olive's Ocean.* Greenwillow Books, 2003. When a school friend dies unexpectedly, Olive seeks a way to commemorate her. Over the course of a memorable summer, Olive will fall in love, be betrayed by her first love, and learn more about her family than she dared imagine. Newbery Honor winner. (INT/MS)

Hesse, Karen. *Witness.* Scholastic Press, 2001. A brilliantly conceived and written novel which uses nine points of view to tell about the Klan's arrival in a New England town in the 1900s. This is a novel in verse. (MS)

Hiaasen, Carl. *Flush.* Alfred A. Knopf, 2005. Noah and Abbey are searching for proof that a floating casino is polluting the waters by having the toilets flush directly into them. (INT/MS)

Hiaasen, Carl. *Hoot.* Alfred A. Knopf, 2002. Roy is new to Florida. A runaway boy, some burrowing owls, and two bullies will ensure that his new town is a memorable one. (MS)

Hite, Sid. *Stick and Whittle.* Scholastic Signature, 2001. An Old West adventure featuring two unlikely protagonists is sure to tickle funny bones. This western with some tall-tale elements makes the book a great read-aloud. (MS)

Hobbs, Will. *Jason's Gold.* HarperTrophy, 2000. Jason follows in the tracks of his older brothers who have headed to the Klondike in search of gold. This riveting adventure and survival story will be very popular with fans of Hobbs—and Paulsen as well. (MS/MMR)

Hoffman, Mary. *Stravaganza: City of Masks.* Bloomsbury, 2002. A young boy with cancer time-travels to an alternate universe where he meets with intrigue and adventure. There are two sequels to this novel. (MS)

Holm, Jennifer L., and Matthew Holm. *Baby Mouse: Queen of the World!* Random House, 2005. This graphic novel introduces readers to BabyMouse, who adores pink and hates volleyball. (INT)

Holt, Kimberly Willis. *My Louisiana Sky.* Holt, 1998. Tiger knows her parents are different. When her glamorous aunt arrives, she offers Tiger a chance to leave home and start a new life. (INT/MS)

Holt, Kimberly Willis. *When Zachary Beaver Came to Town.* Holt, 1999. Zachary Beaver is billed as the world's fattest boy. His arrival in a small Texas town creates quite a stir one summer. Before the summer is ended, there will be a baptism, a funeral, and a disappearance. National Book Award winner. (INT/MS)

Holt, Kimberly Willis. *Dancing in Cadillac Light.* Putnam, 2001. Whenever life closes in on Jaynell, she simply climbs inside one of the cars in the local parts junkyard. (MS)

Horvath, Polly. *Everything on a Waffle.* Farrar, Straus and Giroux, 2001. Newbery Honor book for 2002 tells about Primrose and her woes after her parents are lost at sea. (INT)

Howe, James, and Deborah Howe. *Bunnicula.* Atheneum, 1979. Chester, the hysterical cat owned by the Monroe family, is certain that the new pet rabbit is actually a vampire. How can Chester convince Harold the dog to assist him in ridding the house of this potentially deadly creature? Also in the series: *The Celery Stalks at Midnight, Howliday Inn,* and *Nighty-Nightmare.* (INT)

Howe, James (ed). *The Color of Absence: Twelve Stories About Loss and Hope.* Simon Pulse, 2003. Twelve stories about loss and grief by some of the best YA authors around. Included in the collection are: Avi, Naomi Nye, Angela Johnson, and Chris Lynch. (MS/MMR)

Howe, James. *The Misfits.* Atheneum, 2001. Sticks and stones may break my bones, but names will break my spirit. Howe explores the lives of four friends who decide to take a stand against name calling. The companion novel, *Totally Joe,* provides readers with more insight into one of the characters from this book. (INT/MS)

Jacques, Brian. *Redwall.* Putnam, 1986. This is the first of the Redwall animal adventure series in which a group of plucky animals undertake dangerous quests and adventures. This is high animal fantasy by one of the best. (INT/MS)

Janeczko, Paul B. (ed.). *Seeing the Blue Between: Advice and Inspiration for Young Poets.* Candlewick Press, 2002. Poets offer advice and poems for young writers. (MS)

Janeczko, Paul B. *Top Secret: A Handbook of Codes, Ciphers, and Secret Writing.* Candlewick Press, 2004. Want to communicate in secret? Make invisible ink? Solve cryptological puzzles? This book can help. (INT/MS)

Jennings, Patrick. *The Wolving Time.* Scholastic Press, 2003. Laszlo longs for the time when he will be old enough to join his parents when they morph into their wolf personas. (MS)

Johnson, Angela. *Bird.* Dial Books, 2004. Novel told from three points of view that intersect nicely to bring the story to a conclusion. (MS)

Kadohata, Cynthia. *Kira-Kira.* Atheneum, 2004. Katie watches her beloved fourteen-year-old sister struggle with cancer. This Newbery Medal winner explores themes of family, rivalry, and racism. (INT/MS)

Kerr, M. E. *Slap Your Sides.* HarperCollins, 2001. It's tough when all the young men around you are enlisting to fight in World War II and you remain a conscientious objector. Also by the author: *Dinky Hocker Shoots Smack, I'll Love You When You're More Like Me.* (MS/MMR)

Klass. David. *You Don't Know Me.* Farrar, Straus and Giroux, 2001. Though the book deals with the serious topic of abuse, the humorous narrative of the protagonist provides much needed comic relief. (MS/MMR)

Konigsburg, E. L. *Silent to the Bone.* Atheneum, 2000. Who killed Baby Nikki? Her half-brother, Branwell, is in jail as the number one suspect. His best friend is anxious to prove Bram's innocence. The companion book to this novel is *The Outcasts of 19 Schuyler Place.* (INT/MS)

Korman, Gordon. *Nose Pickers from Outer Space.* Hyperion, 1999. The first book in a series features the exploits of Stan from the planet Pan. His computer is, unfortunately, in his nose and so he is forced to send messages to his home planet by placing his finger in his nose on a regular basis. (INT)

Korman, Gordon. *Maxx Comedy: The Funniest Kid in America.* Hyperion, 2003. Max wants to win a stand-up comedy competition for kids. Only trouble is, he cannot find an audience to appreciate his comic genius. Other books by this author include *This Can't Be Happening at MacDonald Hall, No More Dead Dogs, Island,* and *The Zucchini Warriors.* (INT/MS)

Leavitt, Martine. *Heck, Superhero.* Hyperion, 2003. Heck's mother tends to lose herself from time to time. He has learned to fend for himself, but this time he feels as if his whole world is crumbling. (MS)

Levine, Gail Carson. *Cinderellis and the Glass Hill.* HarperCollins, 2000. Cinderellis is the youngest of three brothers. He enters a contest to win the hand of a beautiful princess. Other titles in this series about princesses include: *The Fairy's Return, The Fairy's Mistake,* and *The Princess Test.* (INT/MS)

Levy, Constance. *Splash: Poems of Our Watery World.* Orchard Books, 2002. Lovely, lyrical poems and light verse about water in its various states. (INT/MS)

Levy, Elizabeth. *Seventh-Grade Tango.* Hyperion, 2001. The new dance class at school might just be more interesting than the students first thought. The new teacher certainly is cute. (MS)

Littman, Sarah Darer. *Confessions of a Closet Catholic.* Dutton, 2005. Her parents don't know that Justine decides to give up Judaism and try Catholicism. She hides in the closet and confesses to Father Ted. (MS)

Lobel, Anita. *No Pretty Pictures: A Child of War.* Greenwillow Books, 1998. An autobiography that shows how a young girl and her family survived during the Holocaust. (MS/MMR)

Lowry, Lois. *Messenger.* Houghton Mifflin, 2004. The final book in the *Giver* story (second book: *Gathering Blue)* brings the story full circle. See what happens to Jonas and Kira. (MS/MMR)

Lubar, David. *Flip.* Starscape TOR, 2003. When Taylor and Ryan find some mysterious disks, little do they think that they will be off on some grand adventures. Also by the author: *Invasion of the Road Weenies, Sleeping Freshmen Never Lie, In the Land of the Lawn Weenies and Other Misadventures.* (MS/MMR)

Lynch, Chris. *Extreme Elvin.* HarperTrophy, 1999. Remember Elvin, from *Slot Machine*? He is back and trimmed down a bit and having to deal with dances, girlfriends, hemorrhoids, and other unspeakable challenges. (MS/MMR)

Lynch, Chris. *Gold Dust.* HarperCollins, 2000. Two boys become friends one spring even though they do not share the same culture. Baseball binds them in more ways than one. (MS/MMR)

Lynch, Chris. *The Gravedigger's Cottage.* HarperCollins, 2004. Two children worry when their father lapses into unusual behavior. It's bad enough living in the old gravedigger's cottage. (INT/MS)

Mack, Tracy. *Drawing Lessons.* Little, Brown, 2000. How do you deal with abrupt changes in your life? Does art help heal? (MS)

MacLachlan, Patricia. *Sarah, Plain and Tall.* HarperTrophy, 1987. In lyrical prose, MacLachlan tells of the arrival of mail-order bride Sarah, a young woman who will change the lives of Anna and Caleb and their father. Sequels include *Caleb's Story* and *Skylark.* (INT)

Martin, Ann M. *Here Today.* Scholastic, 2005. Ellie (short for Eleanor Roosevelt Dingman) faces obstacles at home and at school. Her mother, Doris Day Dingman, seems to be at the center of all the struggles. (INT/MS)

Mass, Wendy. *Leap Day.* Little, Brown, 2004. Josie Taylor is celebrating her fourth birthday as a Leaper (someone born on February 29). The day will hold many surprises for her and her family and friends. (MS/MMR)

Mazer, Norma Fox. *What I Believe.* Harcourt, 2005. This novel in verse follows Vicki as she and her parents are forced to move from their comfortable suburban home to a cramped apartment after her father loses his job. (MS)

McKissack, Patricia. *To Establish Justice: Citizenship and the Constitution.* Knopf, 2004. An examination of rights for various groups including people of color, homosexuals, the disabled, and others. (MS/MMR)

McNamee, Graham. *Sparks.* Dell Yearling, 2003. Last year, Todd was in a special needs class. Now in a regular fifth-grade class, he struggles to deal with the name-calling by some of his peers and the challenges of being in a regular classroom. (INT)

McWilliams, Kelly. *Doormat.* Delacorte Press, 2004. Jaime is used to being a doormat. When her friend, Melissa, becomes pregnant at fourteen, Jaime's life changes radically. (MS)

Moore, Martha A. *Matchit.* Dell Yearling, 2002. Matchit is left at an auto graveyeard when his father takes off for a fling with a waitress. He finds a real sense of family in the most unusual place. (INT/MS)

Moriarty, Jaclyn. *The Year of Secret Assignments.* Scholastic, 2005. Told entirely in letters and e-mails, this look at a pen-pal program examines two different schools that are rivals. (MS/MMR)

Murphy, Rita. *Night Flying.* Dell Laurel-Leaf, 2000. Winner of the Delacorte Press Prize for 2000, this is a remarkable coming-of-age story in which a young girl discovers that she, too, possesses special abilities. (MS/MMR)

Myracle, Lauren. *The Fashion Disaster That Changed My Life.* Dutton, 2005. When Alli "wears" a pair of her mother's underwear stuck to her sweat pants at school, she becomes the target of Jeremy's taunts. Surprisingly, the most popular girl in school comes to her defense. (INT/MS)

Naylor, Phyllis Reynolds. *Shiloh.* Atheneum, 1991. Shiloh follows Marty home and his father makes him return the dog even though the owner beats him, but Shiloh runs away again. How can Marty manage to keep Shiloh for his own? There are sequels to this book that follow the further adventures of Marty and Shiloh. Don't forget the movie tie-in. (INT/MS)

Naylor, Phyllis Reynolds. *Jade Green: A Ghost Story.* Atheneum, 2000. Spooky Gothic thriller with great read-aloud potential tells of the fate of a young girl who must go to live with a distant cousin in a home rumored to be haunted. (MS)

Nelson, Theresa. *Ruby Electric.* Atheneum, 2003. Ruby fancies herself a would-be screenwriter. Since her life is not terribly exciting, Ruby uses screenwriting techniques to bring more excitement to her existence. The text of the story fluctuates between a traditional narrative and the screenplay of Ruby's life. (MS)

Nixon, Joan Lowery. *Ghost Town: Seven Ghostly Stories.* Delacorte, 2000. Stories set in actual ghost towns with great bibliographic information for more details, these are ideal for read-aloud. Nixon remains the queen of mysteries for YA readers. (INT/MS)

Nixon, Joan Lowery. *The Making of a Writer.* Delacorte Press, 2002. Autobiography of the queen of mysteries for YA readers. (INT/MS)

Nixon, Joan Lowery. *Nightmare.* Delacorte Press, 2003. A return to summer camp causes Emily's nightmares to grow stronger and more disturbing. Be sure to investigate all the dozens of YA mysteries penned by this talented author including *Whispers from the Dead, Secret Silent Screams, The Name of the Game Was Murder, Spirit Seeker, Who Are You?* (MS)

Nye, Naomi Shihab. *Nineteen Varieties of Gazelle: Poems of the Middle East.* Greenwillow Books, 2002. Nye proves again why she is an acclaimed poet in this collection of poems about people and war and peace. (MS/MMR)

Nye, Naomi Shihab. *A Maze Me: Poems for Girls.* Greenwillow Books, 2005. Tween girls are the subject and target of this collection of poems. (INT/MS)

Oates, Joyce Carol. *Big Mouth and Ugly Girl.* HarperTempest, 2002. An unusual friendship sparks when Ugly Girl stands up for what is right. (MS/MMR)

O'Keefe, Susan Heyboer. *Death by Eggplant.* Roaring Brook Press, 2004. Bertie wants to become a famous chef. His teachers and parents want him to pass eighth grade. His archenemy wants him to die. (MS)

Osborne, Mary Pope. *Hour of the Olympics.* Scholastic, 1998. Jack and Annie are transported via the Magic Tree House to the time of ancient Greece. There they are witness to the first Olympic games. Part of The Magic Treehouse book series, this easy-to-read chapter book entertains and teaches kids about history. (INT)

Paolini, Christopher. *Eragon.* Knopf, 2003. The first in a proposed trilogy follows the exploits of young Eragon, who discovers a mysterious blue stone that suddenly hatches revealing a sapphire-blue dragon inside. Eragon is destined to become a dragon rider and save the endangered dragons from their enemies. Book Two is entitled *Eldest.* (INT/MS)

Paterson, Katherine. *Bridge to Terabithia.* HarperCollins, 1977. This story of an unlikely friendship is a classic of children's literature. Jess and Leslie share a magical kingdom out in the woods near their home. (INT)

Paterson, Katherine. *The Same Stuff as Stars.* Clarion Books, 2002. Jolted from their home and abandoned by their mother, two children must find a way to make a home for themselves with their grandmother. (MS)

Paulsen, Gary. *Hatchet.* Atheneum Books for Young Readers, 1987. The first in a series of exciting adventures about Brian, who survived a plane crash in the wilderness. *Brian's Return* follows. (INT/MS)

Paulsen, Gary. *The Boy Who Owned the School.* Bantam Doubleday Dell, 1991. Jacob is roped into helping out on the school play by his English teacher who does not know better than to allow Jacob the klutz to run the new fog machine. (INT/MS)

Paulsen, Gary. *Alida's Song.* Dell Yearling, 1999. This story is a lovely sequel to *The Cookcamp.* (INT/MS)

Paulsen, Gary. *Tucket's Travels: Francis Tucket's Adventures in the West, 1847–1849.* Dell Yearling, 2003. Francis is heading west on a wagon train when he is kidnapped by Pawnees. Over the course of years, he searches for his family in this action-packed series. (INT/MS)

Paulsen, Gary. *The Quilt.* Dell Yearling, 2005. Gary's childhood memories of his grandmother Alida and a special family quilt are the focus of this evocative memoir. (INT/MS/MMR)

Peake, Mervyn. *Figures Of Speech.* Candlewick Press, 2003. Illustrated versions of some familiar sayings will provide some nice visual puzzles for readers. (MS/MMR)

Peck, Richard. *Unfinished Portrait Of Jessica.* Delacorte Press, 1991. After visiting her father in Mexico, Jessica learns to appreciate her mother. (MS)

Peck, Richard. *A Year Down Yonder.* Dial, 2000. Sequel to the Newbery Honor–winning, *A Long Way from Chicago,* this book won the Newbery Medal. (MS)

Peck, Richard. *The River Between Us.* Dial, 2003. Peck's latest venture into history is lyrical and haunting and examines an aspect of the Civil War not often found in books for younger readers. (MS)

Peters, Julie Anne. *Define "Normal".* Little, Brown, 2000. The peer counseling program may help two young women from very different backgrounds who each need help and support. (MS/MMR)

Peters, Julie Anne. *Luna.* Little, Brown, 2004. A ground-breaking book that sensitively deals with the transgender issue centers around Liam, a young man who knows he was born into the wrong body. Luna, as Liam prefers to be called, longs for the freedom to express his true identity to others. (MMR)

Philbrick, Rodman. *Rem World.* Blue Sky Press, 2000. Neat little sci-fi tale about a young boy's determination to change his life examines what can happen when we sleep. (MS)

Philbrick, Rodman. *The Last Book in the Universe.* Blue Sky Press, 2000. Based on a short story, this futuristic story tells of the importance of having books and readers. Be certain to share the story from Michael Cart's *Tomorrowland* that gave rise to this novel. (MS)

Pilkey, Dav. *The Adventures of Super Diaper Baby.* Scholastic, 2002. Those wonderful young men from the Captain Underpants books have created a new superhero and a nasty villain. Watch out as reluctant readers grab this one off the shelves at breakneck speed. (INT/MS)

Pilkey, Dav. *Captain Underpants and the Big, Bad Battle of the Bionic Booger Boy, Part 1: Night of the Nasty Nostril Nuggets.* Blue Sky Press, 2002. The title says it all for this comic graphic novel, part of the popular series. See the other titles in the Captain Underpants series. (INT/MS)

Proimos, James. *If I Were in Charge the Rules Would Be Different.* Scholastic Press, 2002. This collection of poems, reminiscent of Silverstein, Dahl, and Prelutsky, will be a welcome addition for intermediate libraries. (INT)

Pullman, Philip. *I Was a Rat!* Knopf, 2000. Cinderella from another point of view. What would happen if one of the rats, changed into a page, was not changed back? Tie to *Cinderella's Rat* by Susan Meddaugh and other Cinderella variants. (INT/MS)

Rennison, Louise. *Angus, Thongs, and Full Frontal Snogging: Confessions of Georgia Nicolson.* HarperCollins, 2000. Coming-of-age story set in England but with plenty of appeal on this side of the pond. "Snogging" is kissing, by the way. There are plenty of sequels, too. (MS/MMR)

Rice, David. *Crazy Loco.* Speak, 2003. This collection of stories, set in the Rio Grande Valley, covers the gamut from pets to relatives to school, all with a fresh new outlook. (MS/MMR)

Riordan, Rick. *The Lightning Thief.* Hyperion, 2005. Percy Jackson is a demigod, the son of one of the gods of Mount Olympus. Little does he know the dangers he will face when the other gods learn of his existence. (INT/MS)

Ritter, John H. *Over the Wall.* Philomel Books, 2000. Powerful story of a young man whose obsession with being the best brings out the worst in him on the baseball field is lyrical in its prose. Also by this author: *Choosing Up Sides* and *The Boy Who Saved Baseball.* (MS/MMR)

Rowling, J. K. *Harry Potter and the Half-Blood Prince.* Scholastic, 2005. If you have not read all the books in this series, you are missing a lot. *Harry Potter and the Sorcerer's Stone, Harry Potter and the Chamber of Secrets, Harry Potter and the Prisoner of Azkaban, Harry Potter and the Goblet of Fire, Harry Potter and the Order of the Phoenix.* (INT/MS).

Ryan, Pam Muñoz. *Esperanza Rising.* Scholastic, 2002. Esperanza has led a life of wealth. However, her father's murder leaves Esperanza and her mother with no choice but to flee to the United States and begin life anew as migrant farm workers. (INT/MS)

Ryan, Pam Muñoz. *Becoming Naomi Leon.* Scholastic, 2004. Naomi Leon has had a fairly quiet life until her mother appears out of nowhere one day to reclaim her role in Naomi's life. (MS)

Rylant, Cynthia. *The Heavenly Village.* Scholastic Signature, 2002. Between Heaven and Earth is a resting spot for those souls not yet ready for the final journey. Here are their stories. (ALL)

Rylant, Cynthia. *Boris.* Harcourt, 2005. In nineteen free-verse poems, we get to know Boris the cat. (ALL)

Salisbury, Graham. *Lord of the Deep.* Delacorte Press, 2001. Mikey works the fishing boat with his stepfather, Bill. He wants so much to learn the ropes, to become a good fisherman. (MS)

Schmidt, Gary. *Lizzie Bright and the Buckminster Boy.* Clarion Books, 2004. Turner sees a different side of a small Maine town when he meets Lizzie. Newbery Honor winner. (MS)

Scieszka, Jon. *The Not-So-Jolly Roger.* Penguin, 2004. Fred, Sam, and Joe travel via a magic book back to the time of the pirates. This short and humorous chapter book is part of The Time Warp Trio series and includes titles such as *The Good the Bad and the Goofy, Summer Reading Is Killing Me,* and *Tut Tut.* (INT)

Shan, Darren. *Cirque Du Freak: A Living Nightmare.* Little, Brown, 2001. Darren is lured to an abandoned house one evening to see what is billed as a one-of-a-kind freak show. What he sees that night alters the course of his life and of those he loves most (sequel: *The Vampire's Assistant*). The third book is *Tunnels of Blood;* the fourth is *Vampire Mountain.* By now, there should be ten in the series. (INT/MS).

Shreve, Susan. *Trout and Me.* Dell Yearling, 2004. Two ADD kids help one another. (MS)

Shusterman, Neal. *Downsiders.* Simon & Schuster Books for Young Readers, 1999. Neat sci-fi story about those who live under the streets and what happens when they need the help of those living topside is one sure to entertain readers. Look for other books by Shusterman such as *Full Tilt* and *Dread Locks.* (MS/MMR)

Soto, Gary. *Fearless Fernie: Hanging Out with Fernie and Me.* G. P. Putnam's, 2002. This collection of poems details the friendship between two boys. (MS)

Spinelli, Jerry. *Loser.* HarperTrophy, 2003. Zinkoff has always been a loser at school. However, being a loser does not seem to bother him much. (INT/MS)

Spinelli, Jerry. *Wringer.* HarperCollins, 1998. On the eve of his tenth birthday, the life of Palmer is changed by the appearance of a pigeon on his windowsill. How can Palmer become a wringer if he has a pet pigeon? (INT/MS)

Spinelli, Jerry. *Stargirl.* Knopf, 2000. Popularity or banishment? How will the students treat the astonishingly different new girl at school? (MS/MMR)

Spinelli, Jerry. *Milkweed.* Knopf, 2003 Misha, a fugitive orphan in Poland, is sent to the Warsaw ghetto along with other Jews and gypsies. He manages to forage for food to keep friends and his adopted family alive during their captivity. (MS)

Stanley, Diane. *A Time Apart.* HarperTrophy, 1999. When her mother falls ill, thirteen-year-old Ginny is sent to live with her father in England. Her father, however, has agreed to join a re-creation of a Stone Age community, and Ginny finds herself an unwitting member of this community as well. (MS/MMR)

Stine, R. L. *Rotten School 1: The Big Blueberry Barf-Off.* Scholastic, 2005. Meet Bernie Bridges, a fourth grader who riles his school, the Rotten School, that is. Bernie and his pals Feenman and Crench are constantly on the prowl for ways to pull pranks and get away with as little work as possible. Loads of tongue-in-cheek humor make this a perfect prereading for books such as Korman's MacDonald Hall series. (INT)

Testa, Maria. *Almost Forever.* Candlewick Press, 2003. In this novel told in verse, a young girl's father is sent off to serve in Vietnam. (INT/MS)

Testa, Maria. *Becoming Joe DiMaggio.* Candlewick Press, 2002. Novel told in verse about a grandfather and his grandson who share a passion for listening to baseball on the radio during the forties. (INT/MS)

Thomas, Rob. *Green Thumb.* Simon & Schuster, 2000. Finally, a middle-grade novel from the pen of someone who knows how to deal with bullies and gifted kids in middle school. (MS)

Thompson, Julian. *The Grounding of Group Six.* Avon Books, 1992. What would happen if your parents wanted you dead? (MS/MMR)

Thoms, Annie (ed.). *With Their Eyes: September 11th—The View from a High School at Ground Zero.* HarperTempest, 2002. This is a play put together from the firsthand accounts of 9-11. (MS/MMR)

Turner, Ann. *Learning to Swim: A Memoir.* Scholastic, 2000. Poems tell of an horrific summer of abuse and the beginning of the healing process provide for powerful memoir writing by the author. (MS/MMR)

Vande Velde, Vivian. *Never Trust a Dead Man.* Harcourt Brace, 1999. Winner of the Poe Award for best mystery, this story combines history and mystery with some great good humor. Other recommended books by this author include *The*

Rumplestiltskin Problem, Heir Apparent, and *Magic Can Be Murder.* (MS)

Vande Velde, Vivian. *Three Good Deeds.* Harcourt, 2005. Howard is turned into a goose after he upsets a local witch. In order to be changed back into a boy, he must perform three good deeds. That is not easy when you cannot see in front of your own beak and the only sound people hear when you speak is "honk." (INT/MS)

Voigt, Cynthia. *Izzy Willy-Nilly.* Simon Pulse, 2005. When a cheerleader loses her leg in an accident, she learns there is much more to life. (MS/MMR)

Weeks, Sarah. *So B. It.* HarperCollins, 2005. Heidi's mother is mentally disabled. Thanks to an agoraphobic neighbor, she has been able to lead a fairly normal life until now. (MS/MMR)

Weiss, Jerry, and Helen Weiss (eds.). *Lost and Found.* Forge, 2000. This collection of short stories is based on the real-life experiences of the authors. Check out the story by author John Scieszka entitled "Thirteen Diddles," thirteen variations on a familiar nursery rhyme. (MS/MMR)

Weston, Martha. *Act I, Act II, Act Normal.* Roaring Brook Press, 2003. Topher is tapped to play Rumplestiltskin in the school play with amusing results. (INT/MS)

Whipple, Laura. *If the Shoe Fits: Voices from Cinderella.* McElderry Books, 2002. Cinderella told in verse from multiple perspectives. (MS/MMR)

White, Ruth . *Memories of Summer.* Farrar, Straus and Giroux, 2000. In 1955, Lyric moves with her father and older sister, Summer. Summer's erratic behavior worsens, and Lyric must come to terms with losing her sister and best friend. Also by this author, *Belle Prater's Boy.* (MS/MMR)

Williams, Lori Aurelia. *When Kambia Elaine Flew in from Neptune.* Simon Pulse, reprint edition, 2001. This powerful story of abuse and neglect and hope is intense. (MS/MMR)

Williams, Lori Aurelia. *Broken China.* Simon & Schuster, 2005. China Cup loses her baby daughter suddenly. In her grief, she makes several life-altering decisions that affect her family and friends. (MS/MMR)

Williams, Vera B. *Amber Was Brave, Essie Was Smart.* Greenwillow, 2001. A story of two sisters told in poems and pictures. (INT/MS)

Wolff, Virginia Euwer. *True Believer.* Simon Pulse, 2002. This is a long-awaited sequel to *Make Lemonade.* More books about LaVaughn are to follow. National Book Award and Printz winner. (MS/MMR).

Woods, Brenda. *Emako Blue.* G. P. Putnam's Sons, 2004. Multiple narrators tell of the miraculous and too-short life of one of their classmates. (MS)

Wrede, Patricia. *Dealing With Dragons.* Harcourt, 2002. Cimorene is a princess with a problem: she is bored and does not wish to marry a boring prince. She sets off on a journey to the dragon lair, promising herself as their slave in exchange for room and board. This is the first book in the Enchanted Forest Chronicles. (INT/MS)

bibliography

Professional Works

Allen, Janet. 2004. *Tools for Teaching Content Literacy.* Portland, ME: Stenhouse.

Anderson, Richard C., Elfreida Hiebert, Judith Scott, and Ian Wilkinson. 1985. *Becoming a Nation of Readers.* Washington, DC: National Institute of Education.

Atwell, Nancie. 1989. *In the Middle: Writing, Reading, and Learning with Adolescents.* Portsmouth, NH: Boynton/Cook.

Beers, Kylene. 2005. Reaching Struggling Readers: Presentation for Yale School Development Program Adolescent Literacy Institute, June.

————. 2003. *When Kids Can't Read: What Teachers Can Do.* Portsmouth, NH: Heinemann.

————. 1990. Choosing not to read: An ethnographic study of seventh-grade aliterate students. Unpublished doctoral dissertation. University of Houston, Houston, Texas.

Carlsen, G. Robert, and Anne Sherrill. 1988. *Voices of Readers: How We Come to Love Books.* Urbana, IL: NCTE.

Copeland, Matt. 2005. *Socratic Circles: Fostering Critical and Creative Thinking in Middle and High School.* Portland, ME: Stenhouse.

Daniels, Harvey. 2001. *Literature Circles: Voice and Choice in Book Clubs and Reading Groups.* Portland, ME: Stenhouse.

Donelson, Kenneth and Aileen Pace Nilsen. 1996. *Literature for Today's Young Adults.* Scott Foresman.

Gibson, Karen Sue. 2004. Unpublished doctoral dissertation, University of Houston, Houston, Texas.

Giles, Vickey. 2005. Unpublished doctoral dissertation, University of Houston, Houston, Texas.

Hurlbert, Ann. 2003. "Tween-Age Wasteland: Are We Paying Too Much Attention to the Woes of Preadolescence?" *Slate,* August 29. Sandbox. www.slate.com.

Hymnowitz, Kay S. 1998. "Tweens: Ten Going on Sixteen." *City Journal,* autumn. www.city-journal.org/html/issue8_4.html.

Kantrowitz, Barbara, and Karen Springen. "A Peaceful Adolescence." *Newsweek,* April 25, pp. 58–60.

Krashen, Stephen. 2005. http://www.sdkrashen.com/main.php3. Last accessed, December 2005.

————. 2004. *The Power of Reading: Insights from the Research.* Libraries Unlimited.

Lance, Keith Curry. 2005. http://www.lrs.org/impact.asp. Last accessed, December 2005.

Lesesne, Teri S. 2003. *Making the Match: The Right Book for the Right Reader at the Right Time, Grades 4–12.* Portland, ME: Stenhouse.

Livaudais, Mary. 1986. A survey of secondary students' attitudes toward reading motivation activities. Unpublished doctoral dissertation. University of Houston, Houston, Texas.

National Assessment of Educational Progress (NAEP). 2005. "The Nation's Report Card." Accessed online at http://nces.ed.gov/nationsreportcard/reading/results2003/natachieve_g4.asp.

Nizalowski, Edward. Online posting regarding the ongoing debate concerning the reading habits of the American public, LM_NET@listserv.syr.edu. Accessed March 25.

Rief, Linda. 1991. *Seeking Diversity: Language Arts with Adolescents.* Portsmouth, NH: Heinemann.

Rosenblatt, Louise M. 1996. *Literature as Exploration,* 5th Edition. Modern Language Association.

Smith, Frank. 1987. *Joining the Literacy Club: Further Essays into Education.* Portsmouth, NH: Heinemann.

Strauss, Valerie. 2005. "Odds Stacked Against Pleasure Reading." *Washington Post Online,* May 24. www.washingtonpost.com.

Sutton, Roger. 2005. "Parallel Play." *The Horn Book Magazine.* September/October.

Trelease, Jim. 2005. www.trelease-on-reading.com/ Last accessed, December 2005.

————. 2001. *The New Read-Aloud Handbook.* New York: Penguin Books.

Children's Literature

Ash, Russell. *The Top Ten of Everything* series. New York: Dorling Kindersley.

Anonymous. 1982. *Go Ask Alice.* New York: Avon Books.

Bauer, Joan. 2000. *Rules of the Road.* New York: Puffin

————. 1997. *Sticks.* New York: Yearling.

————. 1995. *Thwonk.* New York: Delacorte Books for Young Readers.

Bauer, Marian Dane. 1987. *On My Honor.* New York: Yearling.

Baylor, Byrd. 1985. *Everybody Needs a Rock.* New York: Aladdin.

Blume, Judy. 1989. *Forever.* New York: Pocket.

Buffy the Vampire Slayer series. New York: Simon Spotlight Entertainment.

Cabot, Meg. *The Mediator* series. New York: Avon.

————. *The Princess Diaries* series. New York: HarperCollins.

Cole, Babette. 2000. *Hair in Funny Places.* New York: Hyperion.

Crutcher, Chris. 2005. *The Sledding Hill.* New York: Greenwillow.

Danziger, Paula. 2004. *The Cat Ate My Gym Suit.* New York: Puffin.

————. 1998. *There's a Bat in Bunk Five.* New York: Putnam.

DiCamillo, Kate. 2001. *The Tiger Rising.* Cambridge, MA: Candlewick.

Dunn, Mark. 2002. *Ella Minnow Pea: A Novel in Letters.* New York: Anchor.

Fleischmann, Paul. 1995. *Bull Run.* New York: HarperTrophy.

————. 1991. *Seedfolks.* New York: HarperTrophy.

Freedman, Russell. 2004. *The Voice That Challenged a Nation: Marian Anderson and the Struggle for Equal Rights.* New York: Clarion.

Folkard, Claire, ed. *The Guinness World Records* series. New York: Bantam.

Gantos, Jack. 2001. *Jack on the Tracks: Four Seasons of Fifth Grade*. New York: Farrar, Straus, and Giroux.

———. 1999. *Jack's Black Book: What Happens When You Flunk an IQ Test?* New York: Farrar, Straus, and Giroux.

———. 1997. *Jack's New Power: Stories from a Caribbean Year.* New York: Farrar, Straus, and Giroux.

Giles, Gail. 2004. *Dead Girls Don't Write Letters*. New York: Simon Pulse.

Going, K.L. 2005. *The Liberation of Gabriel King*. New York: Putnam Juvenile.

Goldschmidt, Judy. 2005. *The Secret Blog of Raisin Rodriguez*. New York: Razorbill.

Griffiths, Andy. 2005. *Just Disgusting!* New York: Scholastic.

Gutman, Dan. 2000. *The Kid Who Ran for President*. New York: Scholastic.

Hesse, Karen. 1997. *Out of the Dust*. New York: Scholastic.

Hinton, S.E. 1997. *The Outsiders*. New York: Puffin.

Hoose, Philip. 2004. *The Race to Save the Lord God Bird*. New York: Farrar, Straus, and Giroux.

Janeczko, Paul and Naomi Shihab Nye, eds. 1999. *I Feel a Little Jumpy Around You: A Book of Her Poems and His Poems Collected in Pairs.* New York: Simon Pulse.

Kafka, Franz. 1972. *The Metamorphosis*. New York: Bantam.

Leavitt, Steve and Stephen J. Dubner. 2005. *Freakonomics: A Rogue Economist Explores the Hidden Side of Everything*. New York: William Morrow.

Lester, Julius. 2003. *When Dad Killed Mom*. San Diego: Silver Whistle.

Mackler, Carolyn. 2005. *The Earth, My Butt, and Other Big Round Things*. Cambridge, MA: Candlewick.

Martel, Yann. 2003. *Life of Pi*. San Diego: Harcourt.

Martin, Bill. 1996. *Brown Bear, Brown Bear, What Do You See?* New York: Henry Holt.

Masoff, Joy. 2000. *Oh Yuck! The Encyclopedia of Everything Nasty*. New York: Workman.

McCloskey, Robert. 1941. *Make Way for Ducklings*. New York: Viking Juvenile.

Munsch, Robert. 1986. *Love You Forever*. Richmond Hill, ON: Firefly Books.

Myers, Walter Dean. 1989. *Fallen Angels*. New York: Scholastic.

Osa, Nancy. 2003. *Cuba 15*. New York: Delacorte.

Paulsen, Gary. 1999. *Dogsong*. New York: Simon Pulse.

———. 1995. *Harris and Me*. New York: Yearling.

———. 1999. *My Life in Dog Years*. New York: Yearling.

———. 1995. *Nightjohn*. New York: Laurel Leaf.

———. 2000. *Soldier's Heart : Being the Story of the Enlistment and Due Service of the Boy Charley Goddard in the First Minnesota Volunteers*. New York: Laurel Leaf.

———. 1998. *The Schernoff Discoveries*. New York: Yearling.

———. 2002. *Woodsong*. New York: Aladdin.

Peck, Richard. 2004. *The Teacher's Funeral: A Comedy in Three Parts*. New York: Dial.

Rennison, Louise. 2002. *On the Bright Side, I'm Now the Girlfriend of a Sex God: Further Confessions of Georgia Nicolson*. New York: HarperTempest.

Ruditis, Paul. 2005. *Rainbow Party*. New York: Simon Pulse.

Sachar, Louis. 200. *Holes*. New York: Yearling.

Schwartz, Alvin. *The Scary Stories* series. New York: HarperTrophy.

Scott, Kieren. 2005. *I Was a Non-Blonde Cheerleader*. New York: Putnam.

Smith, Jeff. 2005. *Out From Boneville (Bone)*. New York: Scholastic.

Snicket, Lemony. *A Series of Unfortunate Events* series. New York: HarperCollins.

Sones, Sonya. 2004. *One of Those Hideous Books Where the Mother Dies*. New York: Simon and Schuster.

Soto, Gary. 2005. *The Afterlife*. San Diego: Harcourt.

Spiegelman, Art. 1996. *The Complete Maus: A Survivor's Tale*. New York: Pantheon.

Standiford, Natalie. *The Dating Game* series. New York: Little, Brown.

Stine, R.L. *The Fear Street* series. New York: Simon Pulse.

Tashjian, Janet. 2004. *Vote for Larry*. New York: Henry Holt.

Twain, Mark. 2002. *The Adventures of Huckleberry Finn*. New York: Penguin Classics.

Vande Velde, Vivian. 1998. *Curses, Inc.: And Other Stories*. New York: Laurel Leaf.

———. 2005. *Tales From the Brothers Grimm and the Sisters Weird*. San Diego: Harcourt.

Wiesner, David. 1997. *Tuesday*. New York: Clarion.

Whyman, Matt. 2005. *Boy Kills Man*. New York: HarperTempest.

Woodson, Jacqueline. 2000. *Miracle's Boys*. New York: Putnam.

Zindel, Paul. 2000. *Rats*. New York: Hyperion.